FUN AND EARNEST;

OR,

RHYMES WITH REASON.

By DARCY W. THOMPSON,

AUTHOR OF "NURSERY NONSENSE; OR, RHYMES WITHOUT REASON."

ILLUSTRATED BY CHARLES H. BENNETT.

LONDON:

GRIFFITH AND FARRAN,

(SUCCESSORS TO NEWBERY AND HARRIS,)

CORNER OF ST. PAUL'S CHURCHYARD.

1865.

POOR ROOKY.

" And, while Puss was asleep, came creep, creep, creep,
To where the basket stood."—P. ?.

CONTENTS.

❧

THE CATCHER CAUGHT.

ISHING in a pond a little boy
stood,
  And he hadn't yet learnt to swim;
And that little boy's mother did all
that she could,
  But he *would* stand close to the brim.

And bobbing up and down the float was seen,
  Till at last there came a bite;
And O what a size that fish must have been,
  For the float dipp'd down out of sight.

The fish down below, and the boy at the top,
  Pull'd both with might and main;
And right into the pond the boy went plop,
  And he never was seen again.

Now, had he just minded what was said,
  Or had he but learnt to swim,
He might have caught that fish, instead
  Of that fish's catching him.

POOR ROOKY.

PUSSY-CAT, they say, went to market
one day,
With a basket upon her head ;
With her butter to sell, and her eggs
as well,
And to buy some fish instead.

But the way was long, and the sun was strong,
And heavy was her load ;
So Pussy sat down, half way to the town,
With her basket upon the road.

A little black rook gave a sly little look
From out of a neighbouring wood ;
And, while Puss was asleep, came creep, creep, creep,
To where the basket stood.

B 2

Now, like all of his race, this little scape-grace
    Was full of curiosity ;
So he softly undid the basket-lid,
    To see what he should see.

And right into the butter he fell with a splutter,
    And his wings were greased all over ;
And he smash'd all the eggs with his little black legs,
    When down came the basket-cover.

And Pussy-cat awaking at the sound of the breaking
    Saw the mischief that was done ;
" Well, to-day," says she, " there's no market for me,
    " Now my butter and my eggs are gone."

But guess Rooky's fright when she added, " Tho' to-night
    " I shall have no fish to fry,
" I can very well sup, as a kind of make-up,
    " On a dish of nice ROOK-PIE."

MR. FOX.

FOX and a goose, so stories say,
   Met once by a river-side;
And both were obliged to cross
      that day
   Before the even-tide.

But cold and keen the north-wind blew,
   And made poor Foxy shiver;
He'd catch a cold, he very well knew,
   If he dared to swim the river.

So said he to the goose, " Just give me a ride
   " From this side to the other,
" And all life long, whatever betide,
   " I'll love you like a brother."

So he sat on her back, as you'd sit in a boat,
With his front paws round her neck ;
And of water upon his shiny coat
There wasn't a single speck.

Then says Mr. Fox to that simple bird,
" This is just my time to sup ;
" It perhaps seems odd, but, upon my word,
" I am going to eat you up."

And before poor Goose one step could stir,
Or aloud for help could squall,
Mr. Fox had made his meal of her,
Feathers and bones and all.

But when he had cramm'd as much as he could,
And was thinking how well he had dined,
A pack of hounds tore out of the wood,
With a huntsman bold behind.

And the hounds and the huntsman bold beside
On Foxy made a rush ;
And the hounds eat him up with the goose inside,
And the huntsman got the brush.

THE SWALLOW'S NEST.

WAS underneath a cottage-roof
A swallow used to fix
Her dwelling, warm and weather-
proof,
Of mud and straw and sticks.

Year after year, as spring roll'd round,
The twittering stranger came,
And still to her delight she found
Her little house the same.

Within that cottage lived a boy,
A trouble to his mother;
She used to say, her only joy
Was that she had no other.

That little boy would never care
   For what his mother said :
He used to say, " I'll do whate'er
   " Comes first into my head."

Now, he had often sat intent
   The swallow's nest a-watching,
While she was filling up a rent,
   Or busy with the thatching.

And many a time that boy would be
   Most saucy to his mother ;
He'd say, " I mean to have, you'll see,
   " That nest some day or other."

Yet he from her as often heard
   How wrong it was to take
What might have cost a little bird
   A week or two to make.

One day his mother had gone out,
   To buy herself a bonnet ;
He leans against the water-spout
   A ladder, and mounts on it.

The swallow on the house-top stood;
    The tears ran down her beak;
She tried, as hard as birdie could,
    To move the little sneak.

"Do spare, kind sir, my little home,
    "My all in all," she said;
"My drawing-, and my dining-room,
    "My kitchen and my bed.

" Four eggs are there," and out she burst
    A-sobbing at the words;
" Those little eggs on Monday first
    " Will be four little birds."

But it was of no earthly use
    Her crying and her beggin';
The little wretch he took her house
    With every single egg in.

And off at once he took his prize,
    And hid it in his chest;
" Ah! ah!" said he, "they'll need sharp eyes
    " To find my birdie's nest."

When home at eve his mother came
    She saw the nest was gone ;
She said, " O Tommy, fye for shame !
    " What have you been and done ?"

Said he—with grief be it confess'd
    A child such fibs could tell—
" I saw the cat run with the nest,
    " And drop it down the well."

Of course, his mother could not give
    To such a tale belief;
" I'll know," said she, " ere long I live.
    " Who was the real thief."

That very night, when darkness hid
    The whole house fast asleep,
The swallow down the chimney slid,
    As nimbly as a sweep.

And first she hopp'd upon the bed,
    And gently drew the clothes off;
Then came and stood close by his head,
    And peck'd the little boy's nose off.

Back up the chimney flew the bird ;
The boy sprang on the floor ;
And, I'll be bound, you never heard
A boy so loudly roar.

His mother ran, in fear and haste ;
Said she, " What shall I do ?"
" O make," said he, " a nose of paste,
" And stick it on with glue."

She made a nose, the best she could,
And stuck it on the place ;
But of course the nose was not as good
As *you* wear on your face.

For when that little boy has a cold,
If he dare to sneeze or cough,
His mother has to keep tight hold,
For fear the nose fall off.

Yet, though he's lost his little nose,
His senses have been saved ;
And wilful Tommy daily grows
More modest, well-behaved.

But now, when he's been good so long,
    It sometimes makes him cry,
To think, had he been good when young,
    He'd not be such a GUY.

FARMER GREED.

" The son had a pocket-pistol.
And the farmer had his gun."—P. 13.

FARMER GREED.

NE morn to shoot at little birds
    Went Farmer Greed and his son;
The son had a pocket-pistol,
    And the farmer had his gun.

And they sneak'd from hedge to hedge and shot
    Every bird they could see;
Birds that walk'd upon the ground,
    Or that sat upon the tree;

Rook and raven, linnet, lark,
    Robin, wren, and sparrow;
And they cramm'd them all in a great big bag,
    And wheel'd them home in a barrow.

And some they stew'd, and some they boil'd,
  And the little ones they toasted ;
And some they fried, and some they broil'd,
  And the bigger ones they roasted.

And so day after day pass'd on,
  Till they reach'd the end of spring,
And there wasn't a bird to clear the fields
  Of worm or creeping thing.

And the ground was strewn with worms and grubs,
  And insects great and small ;
Some had at least a hundred legs,
  And some no legs at all.

And all the trees from top to toe
  Were as white as dusty millers ;
You couldn't have seen one speck of green
  For slugs and caterpillars.

And the insects went wherever a blade
  Of grass was to be found ;
And the barley and wheat were nipp'd, as soon
  As they peep'd above the ground.

And round about the farm-house spread
  The famine far and wide;
So the insects thought they would like to see
  What the farm-house held inside.

And, row after row, away they go,
  With a beetle at their head;
And the beetle knock'd at the kitchen-door,
  But the farmer was still a-bed.

So, as nobody open'd the kitchen-door,
  They all went creeping under,
And·they found the pantry full o' good things,
  And the cupboards cramm'd with plunder.

Butter, and cheese, and eggs, and ham,
  And bacon, fat and lean:
They found the farmer's cupboards full,
  They left his cupboards clean.

And when every cupboard was dry and bare,
  And the good things all were done;
That beetle said: "Upstairs in bed
  " Are Farmer Greed and his son."

On tip-toe up the stairs they crept,
  Till they reach'd the bed-room door;
And laughing with glee, the beetle, said he:
  " I can hear the farmer snore."

And in they crept, but what they did,
  Or what it was befell
That cruel old man and that cruel little boy,
  No mortal man can tell.

We only know they both in bed
  That morn lay sleeping sound;
But two night-gowns and an old night-cap
  Was all at noon we found.

Then, O little boys, pray, warning take;
  Remember these last words:
" When you're out for a walk, you must never throw
      stones
  " At the dear little dicky-birds."

WEASEL'S FERRY.

HREE times seven are twenty-one ;
    " Write one, and carry two :
" Well, Johnny, now the first line's
        done,
    " What next are we to do ?"

But Johnny's eyes this while had been
    Sleepy and sleepier growing ;
And, like a nodding Mandarin,
    His little head was going.

Papa then put the slate away,
    And, waking Johnny, said,
"We're tired, I see, of sums to-day,
    "Let's have a tale instead."

c

. Now tales were Johnny's chief delight,
   So at the very mention,
The sleep was off, his eyes were bright,
   And he was all attention.

❧

THE STORY OF THE DUCK, THE PIGEON,
AND THE HEN.

LONG, long ago, (Papa began,)
   In days when birds could talk,
A Duck, a Pigeon, and a Hen,
   Went out to take a walk.

They'd walk'd, at least, ten miles, I'm sure,
   When Ducky said, "Let's see,
"If we have money to procure
   "A dinner for all three."

The Pigeon's purse was rather full,
   The Hen's was rather light;
Says Ducky, "I've got nothing at all,
   "Except an appetite."

WEASEL'S FERRY.

"He dropp'd his oars, and made a start
Right at poor Pigeon's throat."—P. 19.

So on towards Foxy's inn they hied,
    And all got hungry, very;
And at length they reach'd the river-side,
    By Mr. Weasel's ferry.

Says Mr. Weasel, bowing low,
    "One penny is my fee,
"So for three pence all three I'll row
    "Across the river Dee."

The Pigeon kindly paid for all,
    And each one took his seat;
The weather was so fine, a sail
    Was really quite a treat.

But just when to the deepest part
    The rogue had row'd his boat,
He dropp'd his oars, and made a start
    Right at poor Pigeon's throat.

But he was not allow'd to take
    Miss Pigeon unaware;
For she saw him just in time to make
    A spring into the air.

And into the water Ducky, too,
    Head foremost made a dive ;
And Ducky swam, and Pigeon flew,
    And both escaped alive.

But little Henny dared not stir,
    For she could nor fly nor swim ;
So Weasel, he look'd hard at her,
    And she look'd hard at him.

But, as she upwards gazed to take
    Her last look at the light,
The Weasel seized her by the neck,
    And was going to give a bite—

 * * * *

Papa cut short the story here,
    To Johnny's great surprise,
And then lean'd backwards in his chair,
    And fairly closed his eyes.

"Papa, Papa," poor Johnny cried,
    "Do tell me what the Hen did :"
Papa was either sleepified,
    Or else he just pretended.

And what that little Hen befell,
   Or the Weasel, what became of him,
Papa to Johnny would never tell,
   On purpose to make game of him.

And yet Papa was usually
   So very glad to please him :
Can any one, then, tell me why
   He now thought fit to tease him ?

MASTER HARD-TO-PLEASE.

LITTLE boy I knew, who would never, never do
    A single thing his kind mother bid ;
And the stupid little fellow, he was always finding fault
With everything that everybody did.

From his turn-up little nose and his peevish little ways,
    And the cross, cross look upon his face,
You would really have supposed, there was nothing in the world
    Good enough for this little scape-grace.

One day his mother made him a delicious apple-pie,
  Good enough for a lord or a prince,
But he turn'd up his nose so very, very high,
  That it's never, never gone down since.

And the ragged little boys, and the ragged little girls,
  In the street wherever he goes,
Run after him and cry: "Here *is* a jolly Guy,
  " Here's a chap with a turn'd-up nose !"

THE TWO BROTHERS:

A BOY'S BALLAD.

PART I.—COURTESY.

TWO children, in a cottage bred,
    Were sons of one dear, loving
        mother;
    Such opposites, you'd ne'er have
        said,
That Robert had been Arthur's brother.

Robert was dark; his temper high;
    His hair crisp'd into short, black curls;
Arthur was fair, and mild, and shy,
    With flaxen ringlets like a girl's.

But still their mother used to boast,
  She could not tell of one or other,
Which loved his little comrade most,
  Or which was fondest of his mother.

These brothers on a day in June,
  When blue the sky, and fair the weather,
·Once started in the morning soon,
  To ramble the whole day together.

And far beyond the narrow bound
  Of wonted walk they rambled on,
And halved the length of travell'd ground
  With interchange of talk and fun.

And on they went o'er dale and hill,
  Past meadow green and golden plain,
On stepping-stones o'er running rill,
  Through sun and shade of leafy lane.

On, on, as stranger scenes unroll'd,
  With lengthening hours their pleasure grew;
On, like adventurers of old,
  Pizarro-like, to regions new.

On, careless of the hours, they stroll;
  But travellers hungry grow at last;
So, resting on a grassy knoll,
  They sat and took their noon-repast.

In front a massive gateway stood,
  With herald-griffins carved thereon;
A wood behind; and o'er the wood
  Rose two great towers of frowning stone.

They wonder'd what the towers might be;
  To whom such grandeur might belong;
When, at his ease and saunteringly,
  A peasant whistling came along.

"Stop," Robert cried; "I want to know,
  "Whose are yon stately towers and high?"
The peasant look'd; then whistled low,
  And shrugg'd his shoulders and pass'd by.

But Arthur ran, and said, "My friend,
  "Pray take his words in kindly part;
"My brother spake not to offend;
  "His speech is rougher than his heart."

The peasant look'd in Arthur's face ;
   He took his bonnet in his hand :
" Yon towers belong to Lady Grace,"
   He said, " the towers of Château-grand.

" Now, pardon me, if I advise,
   " Less, Sir, for your sake, than your brother's :
" Who puts a question rudely, ties
   " A padlock on the lips of others."

And Arthur smiled, and turn'd to see
   A touch of red on Robert's face :
"The churl," said Robert, " seems to me
   " But ill to understand his place."

Then made they for the castle-gate ;
   They rang the bell : the warder came :
" Quick, open quick ; I *want* to wait,"
   Said Robert, " on the Castle-Dame."

The man had stood, with keys prepared,
   Behind the gateway to unlock it ;
But, hearing Robert's speech, he stared,
   And dropt the keys back in his pocket.

Said Arthur in his gentle way,
　"Nay, open, kind sir, if you please ;
"We have not always holiday,
　"And few the pleasure-parks like these."

The warder heard : he took his keys :
　Undid the gate, and answer made he ;
"I-WANT may go, but IF-YOU-PLEASE
　"Is welcome to my noble Lady."

But Arthur, he was loth to stir,
　The warder saw, without the other :
"Your winsome face, my little sir,"
　Said he, "shall pass your ruder brother."

So up the winding walk they pass'd,
　Beneath the shade of ancient wood,
And on a smooth lawn came at last,
　And on the lawn the castle stood.

And up a staircase wide of stone
　They pass'd into a spacious hall ;
And shield, and spear, and bow, and gun,
　And antler'd head hung on the wall.

THE TWO BROTHERS.

"I-WANT may go, but IF-YOU-PLEASE
'Is welcome to my noble Lady.'"—P. 28.

On carpet-down, up oaken stair
  They climb: it is a splendid place:
They pass an open door, and there
  Before them sits the Lady Grace.

She rose, and said: "What fortune kind
  Brings me two little guests to-day?"
And Robert said, "We *want* to find
  "Adventures for our holiday."

The Lady Grace, she softly smiled;
  "WANT is," she said, "an ugly word;
"Not often used by gentle child;
  "By gentle Lady never heard."

A blush spread over Robert's face:
  "We came," he said, "to Château-grand,
"To see the wonders of the place,
  "And kiss its gentle Lady's hand."

They kiss'd her hand, upon the ground
  Both brothers kneeling on one knee:
"Ah!" said the Lady Grace, "I've found
  "Two little knights of high degree."

She stoop'd, and kiss'd each little face ;
    She took them kindly by the hand ;
And all the wonders of the place
    She show'd, of her own Château-grand.

From room to room with her they went,
    Where, framed upon the storied wall,
Were ladies fair of high descent,
    And stately warriors, grim and tall.

And Robert said, " These warriors tall
    " Look wondrous grand, but I would rather
" Have one brooch-picture than them all,
    The face of my own soldier-father."

And Arthur said, " Here may we see
    " A-many sweet and gentle faces ;
" But two are sweeter far to me,
    " My Mother's and the Lady Grace's."

And here were mirrors round a room,
    That made a thousand walls of one ;
And sunlight here in curtain'd gloom
    Faintly through colour'd window shone.

And in an old, sequester'd nook,
  That open'd on soft greenery,
Repose, at length, the lady took ;
  The children standing at her knee.

And from the table, clasp'd in gold,
  She rais'd an old tome, vellum-bound,
And turn'd the pictured leaves, that told
  The story of the Table Round.

And here were knights arm'd cap-a-pie,
  At tourney on the tented green ;
And, robed in broider'd cramoisy,
  Were lady fair and stately queen.

As tales of knight and king she read,
  Two names she singled from the rest :
" Where all were brave and good," she said,
  " These were the bravest and the best."

And turning to each listening lad,
  " Those days," she said, " are vanish'd not ;
" Here is my gentle Galahad,
  " And here my fiery Lancelot."

Long sat the lady in the room,
 The children leaning on her knee;
And deeper grew the twilight gloom;
 The pictured leaf you could not see.

And Arthur clung close, close, and heard
 The Lady Grace so gently sigh;
For Arthur's soft, blue eyes had stirr'd
 A sweet, sad, far-off memory.

"Ah! Lady Grace, how sweet you look,
 "So sweet and gentle, that you seem
"A picture in some story-book,
 "Or I am in some pleasant dream."

"Ay, children, I was dreaming too;
 "Which tells me that the hour is late:
"Good-night, my little liegemen true;
 "My carriage waits you at the gate.

"There, children, kiss me on my face;
 "'Tis idle play to kiss my hand:
"Come soon and see your Lady Grace;
 "Your second home is Château-grand."

They rose, and kiss'd her on the face,
    As each had been her loving son ;—
But, strange, how wept the Lady Grace ;
    O how she wept, when they were gone !

"The winsome boy with golden hair,
    "The sweet boy and his bluff, bold brother—
"Ah, Château-grand ! your lady fair
    "Is not as happy as their mother."

Within the parlour, neat and plain,
    That eventide each eager brother
Twice told, and would have told again,
    The day's adventures to his mother.

The mother listen'd, and in fun,
    Or half in fun and half to tease,
Said, "I shall call my elder son,
    "I-WANT ;—my younger, IF-YOU-PLEASE.

"And now, good-night ; but, if you can,
    "When you are cosy-warm in bed,
"Think over what the countryman,
    "The warder, and the lady said.

D

"Their words, I think, dear Robert, shew;
　"And you will think as does your mother;
"That this is true, which long ago
　"I read in some old book or other :—

"'When bolts and bars are in your way,
　"And you are longing to get through them,
"Kind words are found, so wise men say,
　"The key that easiest will undo them.'"

PART II.—LADY GRACE.

Now all the chances that befell
　These brothers, as the years roll'd by,
Were I to try, I could not tell,
　And, could I tell, I scarce should try.

I know that many a time, as sped
　Unnoticed summers o'er the land,
The children took the road that led
　From their own home to Château-grand.

I know their cottage roof and wall
  Rang long with mirth and happy noise;
I know their mother lived to call
  Two gallant youths her bonny boys.

I know that years stole silently
  Upon her, and her hair grew grey :
I know there came an hour when she
  Was call'd of God, and went away.

And then the dear old cottage room,
  So merry in the days of old,
Seem'd curtain'd round and round with gloom ;
  For all the fire, the hearth was cold.

They rose : they took one lingering view :
  They turn'd the key upon the door ;
And O 'twas sad to say "Adieu !
  "Adieu, sweet home, for evermore !"

And so they left the dear, dear place,
  Their child-walk a last time to roam ;
And sought, and found with Lady Grace,
  At Château-grand a second home.

And dearly loved they Lady Grace,
   And still their hearts were fond and true :
An old home and a dear old face
   Were not forgotten for the new.

And Lady Grace, she ne'er forgot ;
   She too had memories sweet and sad ;
But dearly loved she Lancelot,
   And dearly loved her Galahad.

And Arthur took the lady's name ;
   But he alone ; for said his brother ;
" Mine, Lady Grace, must be the same
   " That once my father gave my mother."

That castle was a happy place,
   And pleasant years roll'd swiftly by ;
But thin and pale grew Lady Grace,
   And none could tell the reason why.

Grew thinner, paler, every day ;
   And Arthur never left her side :
At length her call to go away
   Came, and in Arthur's arms she died.

And so one sunny noon were seen
  Two loving brothers bitterly weeping,
Beside two sister-graves grass-green,
  Where two they loved now lay a-sleeping.

And Château-grand was Arthur's now :
  He grew a stately gentleman :
But sadly evermore, I trow,
  Thro' Arthur's brain sweet memories ran.

But Robert, he was still the same :
  His restless spirit chafed with ease :
And so he went to win a name,
  A soldier's name, beyond the seas.

And well he wielded the good sword,
  A soldier in a distant land,
Which once the Lady Grace's lord
  Had wielded in his knightly hand.

And fearless as he was in fight,
  So was he mild with lady near ;
The Bayard of his day ; a knight
  Without reproach and without fear.

But soldier's work, it needeth rest ;
    So, wearied, from that distant land
Came Robert ; and was Arthur's guest,
    A welcome guest, at Château-grand.

THE WITCH'S BOBBIN.

 CHILD sat on the nursery-floor
Beside a broken toy:
" I'll play with baby-things no
more;"
He said : " I'll be a boy."

The silly child in passion spoke :
He turn'd : to his surprise,
An old witch, muffled in a cloak,
Stood there before his eyes.

Her forehead was with wrinkles knit,
And yellow was her skin ;
You'd scarce have put a penny-bit
Between her nose and chin.

" What puts my laddie in a rage ? "
She said : " Why should he cry ? "
He said : " I wish to grow in age :"
She said : " So do not I."

" But if," she said, " such is your mind ;
" If discontent you feel ;
" Here, take this bobbin, and unwind
" The cotton from the reel.

" And every time your fingers ply
" A single yard of thread,
" A year shall fly as silently
" As dream above your head."

A change ! a change ! he pull'd the reel,
Impatient to begin it :
And he has lived, but cannot feel,
Twice five years in a minute.

*   *   *   *

" How very old you look, Papa !
" Your hair and beard are grey :
" And where is dear old grandmama ?
" Why has she gone away ? "

THE WITCH'S BOBBIN.

"What puts my laddie in a rage?'
She said: 'Why should he cry?'"—P. 40.

Papa look'd very stern, and said ;
  " You know as well as I,
" That she has in her grave been laid
  " For years and years gone by.

" A boy should not so idly speak,
  " To cause his father sorrow :
" Go ; learn your Latin and your Greek,
  " The lesson for to-morrow."

His father's words to understand
  The boy is quite unable :
He stares, perplex'd ; and by his hand
  The reel lies on the table.

The change again ! he pulls the thread,
  Impatient to begin it ;
And silently roll o'er his head
  Ten years in half a minute.

     *   *   *   *

The room is still the same ; but see,
  The boy is boy no more :
A prattling child sits on his knee ;
  A cot is on the floor.

Beside him kneels the young Mama,
　　Their baby-boy caressing :
"How sad," she says, " poor Grandpapa
　　" Ne'er lived to see our blessing."

And so for ever out of view
　　Are pass'd two dear old faces :
As dear, maybe a dearer two,
　　Are come to fill their places.

Ah ! happy, happy man ! thy hearth
　　Is bless'd with child and wife :
Such bliss for half an hour is worth
　　A year of other life.

Put by the reel ! such blessed lot
　　To whomsoe'er 'tis given,
He lingers, tho' he knows it not,
　　Hard by the gate of Heaven.

Such hours, alas ! too swiftly fly
　　Without yon fatal skein :
Such hours, when they are once gone by,
　　They never come again.

A something whispers faint and low;
" Home-happiness is tame ;
" Go, mix with those that do and know,
" And win thyself a name!"

The change again! he pulls the thread,
Impatient to begin it ;
And twice five years roll o'er his head
In less than half a minute.

* * * *

A darken'd room : a chill, chill place :
A youth before him stands :
" Who is the youth? why is his face
" Thus buried in his hands?"

He seems with inward grief to shake,
A grief he cannot smother :
" Father, my very heart will break !
" My mother! O my mother!

" Our joy in life is gone away,
" And it will come back never :
" I kiss'd her dear face yesterday,
" And she is gone for ever."

Bewilder'd, with a dull surprise,
　He hears the wild words said :
He stares, and in the gloom descries
　A black thing on the bed.

He trembles, and with both his hands
　He presses hard his brow :
He shrieks—ah ! see, he understands,
　He understands all now.

He cries a loud and bitter cry,
　And falls down in a swound :
Down falls the reel : twice five years lie,
　Unravell'd on the ground.

*　　　*　　　*　　　*

An old man, very pale and wan,
　Lies stretch'd upon a bed :
The witch is at the foot : the son
　Is weeping at the head.

" My son ; how thin I am and weak !
　" How long have I lain sleeping ? "
The son, he tries, but cannot speak,
　Poor loving son, for weeping.

"O put yon beldame to the door!
 "There's death in her cold eye:
"Kiss me, my son; once more; once more;
 "Now, hold me till I die."

The witch heeds not the loving son;
 Heeds not the father's pain :
She says; "Before the day is done,
 "The reel. is mine again.

"My reel, my reel, my magic reel!
 "You pull the fatal thread,
"And swifter than your senses feel,
 "The years roll over head.

"O foolishest of foolish men,
 "To squander life away;
"For thou hast lived threescore and ten
 "Long years in one short day!"

THE MAGIC LANTERN:

OR,

WORDS; WORDS; WORDS.

HE Lady Katharine de Velours,
  She lives in style; and Lady
   Kitty
 Is very learned, and very demure,
  And once, they say, was rather
   pretty.

'Twas she that wrote—but you know that—
 Those books so full of sound advice;
" Cheese-parings for the hungry Rat,"
 And " Traps to catch unwilling Mice."

She wrote those pretty books, I'm told,
 The poor and ignorant to teach;
They're bound in calf, and edged with gold,
 And only cost a guinea each.

Once only I had the honour to get
To Purrleigh Manor an invitation;
To meet a most distinguish'd set
Of noble friends to education.

Sir Foozle Poodle of Berkeley Hall;
Lord Leveret, son of Earl Marchwater;
General Sir Perroquet McCawl,
With pretty Polly, his youngest daughter.

The Manor chaplain, Mr. Rook;
The blushing curate, Mr. Coo;
The great Parsee, Sir Bubble-y-jook,
And squires and M.P.s not a few.

First to the library we went,
Where mental food in store was found,
And half a learned hour we spent
As toast and coffee were handed round.

To microscopes some glued their faces,
Or peer'd at mites or fishes' fins;
And eyed black-beetles, ranged in cases,
Martyrs to science, stuck on pins;

Tadpoles in bottles with wax-seal'd stoppers ;
   Fire-arms in rusty-brown condition ;
Long rows of Greek and Roman coppers,
   Far gone in green decomposition.

Some gazed at flies upon the wall,
   Or pass'd their fingers through their hair,
Or fixedly stared at nothing at all,
   Or languish'd in a mild despair.

The thing was verging on ennui,
   When rang the bell, the guests to call
To where a lecture was to be
   Deliver'd in the servants' hall.

Scarce in our chairs had we lean'd back,
   When up the room came gravely slow,
Be-wigg'd and clad in learned black,
   Signor Dottore Giacomo.

There was, as far as I could tell,
   A something queer in Signor Giaco ;
And as he pass'd, there was a smell
   Of most uncommonly strong tobacco.

The room was dark, but I could see
  A magic lantern on a stand:
The Doctor held what seem'd to me
  A slide of glass in either hand.

Suddenly, in my ears the sound
  Of a shrill squeaky voice was dinning;
And in an hour myself I found
  No wiser than at the beginning.

To understand one single word
  I had been utterly unable;
The Doctor surely, I inferr'd,
  Was fresh from Bedlam or from Babel.

He ceased : a lighted chandelier
  Dispell'd the temporary gloom;
Stifled applause or murmuring cheer
  Of thankfulness ran through the room.

The General rose his legs to stretch,
  Then whisper'd softly to his daughter,
" Tell what's-his-name to go and fetch
  " A glass of something and soda water."

E

Lord Leveret said, " 'Twas twuly gwand,
  " Upon his word, and monstwous pwetty ;"
" And calculated to expand
  " Enquiring minds," said Lady Kitty. ·

A smile half on, half off his lip,
  Said Mr. Rook, " I'm sure all present
" Are grateful to your Ladyship
  " For rendering thus instruction pleasant."

" Ya—as," Sir Foozle Poodle said ;
  " This sawt of magic what-d'ye-may-caw
" Weminds me that I've somewhere wead
  " About this kyind of thing befaw."

Said Lady Kitty, " If that be so,
  " Pray rise and make some observation :
" The shortest lecture would, you know,
  " Confer a very great obligation."

Sir Foozle rose and said : " No doubt,
  " Aftaw, my fwiends, what you have seen,
" You'd like to know a little about
  " The histowy of this stwange machine.

" A man invented this machine
    " A vewy, vewy long while ago;
" A clevah fellah he must have been,
    " But what his name was—I don't know.

" The use is simple, if you knew;
    " You open or you shut this lid;
" You put the slides in; and you do—
    " Exactly what the Signor did.

" The ancient Bwitons, savage men,
    " Knew little or nothing at all about it;
" They had no magic lantern then;
    " But they contwived to do without it.

" And Julius Cæsar, I'll be bound,
    " When first he cwoss'd the sea to Dovah,
" This sawt of thing would not have found
    " If he had search'd all Bwitain ovah.

" Our wude forefathers then, you see,
    " Were not so well off quite as we aw;
" Which is, of course, to you and me
    " A vewy consolatowy ideaw."

With loud applause the servants greet
   The speech : one cheer ! another yet !
The Butler said, " It *was* a treat
   " To hear a real live baronet."

Now I must own a truth unpleasant,
   Which I am blushing to recall ;
The plain fact is, of all then present
   None had seen anything at all.

The learned Signor Giacomo,
   Or, in plain English, Master Jacko,
Had taken, I for certain know,
   Something *besides* his strong tobacco.

So, tho' he possibly had rehearsed
   Descriptions true of every slide,
He had forgotten at the first.
   To light the little lamp inside.

And worthy Giacomo as yet
   Scarce in his speech was ankle-deep
Before my Lady and her set
   Were snoring some, and all asleep.

THE MAGIC LANTERN.

"He had forgotten at the first
To light the little lamp inside."—P. 52.

And those who dared not sleep or snore,
  Staring at nothing, bewilder'd sat,
And might have seen as much, or more,
  If they had stared inside my hat.

And, strange, the only one that had
  Perceived poor Giacomo's quandary,
Was one Bob Dorg, a butcher-lad,
  Sharp as a knife, but vulgar—very.

He had meant to tell the scullery-maid,
  His cousin, of the lecture, after;
But, hearing what the butler said,
  Bob burst into a roar of laughter.

Lord Leveret call'd, " Why, what's the wow ?"
  Poor Lady Kitty was pale with fright;
Sir Foozle said, " It's ovah now;
  " They've kicked him out, and serve him wight."

Perhaps it *did* serve Bobby right;
  For tho' what's false is ne'er allow'd,
Yet, sometimes, 'tis most impolite
  To utter certain truths out loud.

'Tis true enough that Bob's own nose
    Is rather puggy, as you well know;
But would he like, do you suppose,
    Any one else to tell him so?

If Tommy took that liberty,
    Bobby, I think, would feel inclined
To let young Master Tommy see,
    A little of his, Bobby's, mind.

Still, I must own, 'twixt you and me,
    That in my heart I felt a throb
Of warm and genuine sympathy
    For vulgar, ugly, but honest Bob.

And so, whenever a speaker now
    Makes long half hours of every minute,
Havering a kind of bow—wow—wow,
    Dull, pompous stuff with nothing in it;

When words are thick as peas, and thought
    Like currants in school-dumplings spread,
I think, why, surely, *he*'s forgot
    The light inside *his* lantern-head.

TO COUSIN TOMMY;

THE FIRST LETTER FROM OUR NURSERY.

EAR TOMMY, I don't know where
you are,
But I'm told it's far away;
So I'm sitting by Nurse, who is
writing for me,
To tell what I've got to say.

And I've got such a deal to say, Tommy dear,
Such a lot of nice things to show;
I only wish you were here, Tommy dear,
Were it just for a day or so.

I've got a great big tortoise-shell cat,
But Pussy is too well fed;
For she's lazy and fat, and won't catch mice;
But she purrs when I take her to bed.

And a dear little dog that can stand on two legs,
　And he's speckled all black and white;
And I sometimes pull him hard by the tail,
　And he growls, but he daren't bite.

And, O! such a duck of a pony!
　I wish you were here to see;
His coat is rough, and he's very small,
　But his tail is as long as me.

I think he will soon be too little for me,
　And then I shall give him away;
But the person I mean to give him to,
　As yet I don't choose to say.

But perhaps I shall give him to you, Tommy dear,
　As soon as I'm tall and strong;
For then I shall have a big horse to myself,
　And I'll ride about all the day long.

And I'll buy a great three-masted ship,
　And I'll paint it black and red,
And I'll sail it about in the real sea
　Till it's time to go to bed.

TO COUSIN TOMMY.

"And, O! such a duck of a pony!
I wish you were here to see."—P. 56.

Pa' made me a boat himself last week,
  But the boat it was far too small;
It wouldn't hold Puss, if I put her inside,
  And it's got no masts at all.

It was only last week Papa came home;
  He had been away such a long while;
I think I've never once seen him laugh,
  And I seldom see him smile.

But he's very kind and good to me,
  And he gives me lots of toys:
Papa, I suppose, is too clever or old
  To talk with little boys.

The night he came home he was sitting alone,
  And I crept in close by his side;
But he held his face between both hands,
  And you can't think how he cried.

Now, I couldn't tell what they had done to Papa,
  But I thought, if I were as tall,
They might beat me as hard as ever they liked,
  But I'd never cry at all.

For I tumbled in going down stairs one day,
   And it made such a bump on my head;
And in hollowing out my boat, I cut
   My finger until it bled.

But nurse can tell you I didn't cry,
   But I held my two hands fast,
And I bit my lips as hard as I could,
   Until the pain was pass'd.

But it's weary to be so young and so small;
   I mean to do all I can;
I'll go to bed soon, and I'll stand in the rain,
   And I'll try to grow into a man.

TO THE SWALLOW.

 ELCOME, wanderer, to me !
Welcome, early comer !
Hither over land and sea
Thou comest, seeking Summer.

Summer soon will pass away ;
Autumn next will follow ;
Long ere Winter we shall say,
" Good-bye, wandering Swallow !"

A HOLIDAY TO-MORROW.

O you think we shall have to-morrow,
    Papa,
    Sunshine and fair weather ?
You promised, you know, the next
    fine day
We should sail our ship together.

And all last week I worked, Papa,
    As hard as I was able ;
And without a mistake can say "three times"
    In my multiplication table.

So after breakfast to-morrow, Papa,
    We'll go to the water-side,
And launch our wee ship as they launch
    A big ship on the Clyde.

But Pilot must not go with us, Papa,
  That naughty dog, because
Last time he went swimming out after the ship,
  And capsized it with his paws.

But suppose, when our ship were far from the land,
  The wind should come, and. the rain,
And she should go down, down below,
  And never be seen again ?

But no, no, no : no storm shall blow ;
  But the sun will shine all day,
And a soft, soft wind will puff behind,
  And our ship shall sail away.

And I'll sit down by the water-side,
  And Papa shall sit by me ;
And we'll shut our eyes, and make believe
  We are sailing on the sea.

THE WINDS.

THE NORTH-WIND.

HITHER, Papa, does the North-wind
go,
When he's tired of the storm, and
has ceased to blow ?

In cold, blue seas, in a frozen zone,
The monarch sits on a glittering throne ;
A throne of ice that rises on high
With spire and pinnacle into the sky :
With snort and spout of thundering sound
Sea-horse and whale go sailing round :
Wrapt in his winter coat of hair,
Plods thro' the mist the great white bear;
Or prowling alone the fox will go,
White-coated, peaky-faced, over the snow ;
You might stay there a year, and you never would see
Blossom, or flower, or green-leaved tree ;

A year, and the while would never be heard
Voice of man or carol of bird ;
A year, and never would summer sun
That desolate wilderness shine upon :
Glad to escape is the mariner bold,
That has seen yon king in his realm of cold.

THE EAST-WIND.

WHITHER, Papa, when he's tired in the sky,
Whither away does the East-wind fly ?

Yoked to his car, his swift steeds go
Over high mountain-peaks, cover'd with snow ;
Over green Tartar-land onwards they flee,
Plains as vast as the boundless sea ;
Sometimes a horseman on trampling steed
Passes them, riding at galloping speed ;
Sometimes comes trailing a long caravan
Of horse and camel and merchantman ;
Then slowly they all disappear, and again
The car drives over a desolate plain ;

Never a moment that car will stay,
Till it reaches the beautiful gates of Day;
There, rising from out of his ocean-bed,
The great Sun at dawn lifts his glorious head,
And the sky, that before was gray and cold,
Lights up at his coming with crimson and gold.
Some morn, when the world is asleep and still,
Together we'll go to the top of yon hill,
And we'll watch how the darkness goes paling away,
How climbs up the heaven the opening day,
And how the sky glows with a million roses;
And see where the East-wind, when weary, reposes.

THE SOUTH-WIND.

WHEN the warm South-wind is tired with play,
To what far-off home does he hurry away?

Far away, far away, under sunnier skies,
Past the Moon-mountains his resting-place lies;
Flowers are there blooming of every hue,
Crimson and scarlet, yellow and blue;

Flowers of perfume rich and rare,
Scatter'd like weeds o'er the garden fair;
Bright as the rainbow or butterfly's wing,
Fairer in winter than ours in spring.
Fruit there ripens of every kind,
Citron and orange of golden rind;
Melon, whose juice so fresh and sweet
Would cool you under the noon-day's heat;
Clustering grape on drooping vine,
Peach, pomegranate, and nectarine.
But with walls of brass hemm'd round and round
Is the whole of that magical garden-ground;
And watching sleeplessly, early and late,
A dragon sits at the garden-gate,
So that no mortal may ever behold
The wonderful flowers and the fruit of gold.

THE WEST-WIND.

WHEN he's tired with play, and has ceased to blow,
Whither, Papa, does the West-wind go?

F

Far away is an island, emerald-green,
Where mortal mariner ne'er has been;
Meadow-lawns, soft as soft can be,
Slope gently down to the brimming sea;
Over-head hanging, a rich warm air
Makes perpetual summer there.
On the soft meadow-grass, close to the deep,
Are good knights of olden times lying asleep;
Taking their rest till the wounds are heal'd,
Got upon glorious battle-field:
Good King Arthur is sleeping there,
And watching beside him are ladies fair;
The king and his knights of the Table Round
Lie on the meadow-lawn sleeping sound.
At sunset, walk by the sea, and behold
The clouds of purple with fringe of gold;
Like the curtains at night around your bed,
Those clouds round the beautiful isle are spread.
There's a magical ship that sails over the sea,
And the name of that ship is Phantasie;
And over the sea, in some warm, sunny weather,
Papa and his Boy will go sailing together.

THE WILD-BEAST SHOW.

WELL, Grandmama, to the Wild-
beast Show
Nurse and I have been;
So, if you'll let me sit on your knee,
I'll tell you all we've seen.

A leopard we saw, that look'd like a cat,
A great cat cover'd with spots;
I think he was painted with mustard first,
And afterwards spoilt with blots.

And a lion, just like a big yellow dog,
Was glaring behind his bars;
His head seem'd a deal too big, and his beard
Was twice as long as Papa's.

F 2

And a great giraffe, with a little wee tail,
   And a neck so long, Nurse said,
He might have his toes in the kitchen-yard,
   And his nose upstairs in bed.

And swimming about in the water
   Was a great white polar bear;
No wonder he finds the weather too hot,
   With such a thick coat of hair.

And there were such lots of monkeys,
   All sizes, black and brown;
I'm sure they can talk, for they seem'd to me
   Like little black men baked down.

But the great big elephant, Grandmama,
   Seem'd the funniest beast to me;
For he keeps two teeth outside his mouth,
   And a tail where his nose should be.

Nurse call'd it his *trunk*; but a trunk you know
   Is made to hold one's clothes;
Then why put his coat, if he's *got* a coat,
   Inside his tail or his nose?

Now, Pussy and Rab have just one tail,
   And one tail seems to do ;
I suppose, Grandmama, it's because he's so big,
   That an elephant must have two.

Still, if I were an elephant, Grandmama,
   I think I should feel inclined
To keep my teeth inside my mouth,
   And to hang both tails behind.

But I'm sure if all the beasts in the show
   Were offer'd me, great and small,
I wouldn't give Pussy or little Rab dog,
   Or poor Cockatoo for them all.

THE ORGAN-MAN AND THE MONKEY.

COME to the window, Johnny;
  Come as quick as you can;
There's a man with a barrel-organ,
  And a monkey dress'd like a man.

Nurse, you may go to the door,
  And give the poor fellow a penny;
Johnny, we've had a good dinner, you know,
  And perhaps he's not had any.

There—he's got the money;
  See, how he's smiling now;
He's telling the monkey to take off his hat,
  And make us a splendid bow.

THE WILD-BEAST SHOW.

" I wouldn't give Pussy or little Rab dog,
Or poor Cockatoo for them all."—P. 70.

Listen ! he's playing again :
  Do you know what makes the sound ?
There are little wee men that sing inside,
  As he turns the handle round.

Little wee men that sing,
  And frisk inside and caper ;
No bigger they than your finger-nail,
  And as thin as tissue-paper.

Though you should lift the lid
  Softly for fear of fright'ning,
Before you could say " Jack Robinson,"
  They'd be off like a flash of light'ning.

THE WALK TO SCHOOL.

 LITTLE lad one morn in May,
  As like a snail he crept to school,
Saw like a sunbeam flash and play
  A wee fish in a pleasant pool.

Upon the grassy bank to rest
  He sat, and overhead he heard
A *trill-lill* from a little nest
  Piped by some merry morning-bird.

"You swim," he said, "wee shiny fish,
  "Because you've nothing else to do:
"And I would swim, had I my wish,
  "And you should have my sum to do.

"And pretty bird, had I my will,
  "I'd sit like you on yonder tree,
"And sing all day your *trill-a-lill*,
  "And you should learn my A, B, C."

Then up he rose, and went to school;
  A weary, weary way; for still
The fish, he knew, swam in the pool,
  The birdie sang *trill-trill-a-lill*.

LILY'S BALL.

ILY gave a party,
  And her little playmates all,
    Gaily drest, came in their best,
    To dance at Lily's ball.

Little Quaker Primrose,
  Sat and never stirr'd,
And except in whispers
  Never spoke a word.

Tulip fine and Dahlia
  Shone in silk and satin;
Learned old Convolvulus
  Was tiresome with his Latin.

Snowdrop nearly fainted
  Because the room was hot,
And went away before the rest
  With sweet Forget-me-not.

Pansy danced with Daffodil,
  Rose with Violet;
Silly Daisy fell in love
  With pretty Mignonnette.

But, when they danced the country-dance,
  One could scarcely tell
Which of these two danced it best—
  Cowslip or Heather-bell.

Between the dances, when they all
  Were seated in their places,
I thought I'd never seen before
  So many pretty faces.

But of all the pretty maidens
  I saw at Lily's ball,
Darling Lily was to me
  The sweetest of them all.

And when the dance was over,
   They went downstairs to sup ;
And each had a taste of honey-cake,
   With dew in a butter-cup.

And all were dress'd to go away
   Before the set of sun ;
And Lily said "good-bye !" and gave
   A kiss to every one.

And before the moon or a single star
   Was shining overhead,
Lily and all her little friends
   Were fast asleep in bed.

THE LITTLE LOVERS.

ITTLE Boy-sailor with jacket of
    blue,
Fond hearts at home have been
    thinking of you;
Dreaming the long nights, and
    thinking all day
Of a darling boy-sailor, while he was away;
And when the ship sail'd away, oh! how they cried,
Mother and sister, and—some one beside.

Dear little Golden-hair, I will tell thee
What I saw, what I heard on the deep sea;
As I sat all alone on the mast high,
A sea-maiden singing and swimming came by;
Combing her tangled and silken green hair,
Thus she sang sweetly, that sea-maiden fair:

" Little Boy-sailor with jacket of blue,
" Mother and sister are thinking of you;
" He, too, forgets not, where'er he may roam,
" Mother and sister, and sweet, sweet home ;
" But a something makes little Boy-sailor's eyes dim,
"When he's thinking of some one—who's thinking of him."

So she pass'd swimming, and swimming she sang ;
And in mine ears the sweet music still rang ;
And I felt, on the mast sitting alone,
Millions of tiny threads over me thrown ;
Threads by the silk-worm in Fairy-land spun—
I felt them all over, but couldn't see one ;
But I knew that the magic web only could be
Thrown by kind Fairies across the wide sea,
To bind little Golden-hair close, close to me.

A MORNING HYMN.

A, a, a: it is the break of day:
Blithely are the birdies singing,
From their little nests up-springing:
A, a, a: it is the break of day.

E, e, e: how thankful I should be!
Round my bed, as I lay sleeping,
Holy angels guard were keeping:
E, e, e: how thankful I should be!

I, i, i: the Sun is in the sky:
See, his pleasant light comes stealing
Thro' the lattice o'er the ceiling:
I, i, i: the Sun is in the sky.

O, o, o : how soft the breezes blow !
All the pretty flowers awaking
 Dew from little leaves are shaking :
O, o, o : how soft the breezes blow !

U, u, u : our days are short and few :
May each sun to rest a-going
 Find me wiser, better growing :
U, u, u : our days are short and few.

PRINTED BY R. CLAY, SON, AND TAYLOR, LONDON.

ORIGINAL JUVENILE LIBRARY.

A CATALOGUE

OF

NEW AND POPULAR WORKS.

PRINCIPALLY FOR THE YOUNG.

PUBLISHED BY

GRIFFITH AND FARRAN,

(SUCCESSORS TO NEWBERY AND HARRIS),

CORNER OF ST. PAUL'S CHURCHYARD,

LONDON.

WERTHEIMER AND CO., CIRCUS PLACE, FINSBURY CIRCUS.

NEW AND POPULAR WORKS.

THOMAS HOOD'S DAUGHTER.

Crosspatch, the Cricket, and the Counterpane ;
A Patchwork of Story and Song, by FRANCES FREELING BRODERIP. Illustrated by her brother THOMAS HOOD. Super royal 16mo. price 3s. 6d. cloth, 4s. 6d. coloured, gilt edges.

Merry Songs for Little Voices ;
The words by Mrs. BRODERIP; set to music by THOMAS MURBY, author of " The Musical Student's Manual," " The Golden Wreath," etc.; with 40 illustrations by THOMAS HOOD. Fcap. 4to., price 5s. cloth.

THE HONBLE. MISS BETHELL.

Echoes of an Old Bell ;
And other Tales of Fairy Lore, by the Honble. AUGUSTA BETHELL. Illustrations by F. W. KEYL. Super royal 16mo., price 3s. 6d. cloth, 4s. 6d. coloured, gilt edges.

Fun and Earnest ;
Or, Rhymes with Reason, by D'ARCY W. THOMPSON, author of "Nursery Nonsense; or, Rhymes without Reason." Illustrated by CHARLES BENNETT. Imperial 16mo., price 2s. 6d. cloth, 3s. 6d. coloured, gilt edges.

CAPTAIN MARRYAT'S DAUGHTER.

A Week by Themselves ;
By EMILIA MARRYAT NORRIS, with illustrations by CATHARINE A. EDWARDS. Super royal 16mo., price 2s. 6d. cloth, 3s. 6d. coloured, gilt edges.

LADY LUSHINGTON.

Hacco the Dwarf ;
Or, The Tower on the Mountain ; and other Tales, by LADY LUSHINGTON, author of " The Happy Home." Illustrated by G. J. PINWELL. Super royal 16mo., price 3s. 6d. cloth, 4s. 6d. coloured, gilt edges.

The Primrose Pilgrimage.
A Woodland Story, by M. BETHAM EDWARDS, author of " Little Bird Blue," " Holidays among the Mountains," etc., with illustrations by T. R. MACQUOID. Imperial 16mo., price 2s. 6d. cloth, 3s. 6d. coloured, gilt edges.

The Happy Holidays ;
Or, Brothers and Sisters at Home, by EMMA DAVENPORT, author of " Our Birthdays," " Live Toys," etc. Frontispiece by F. GILBERT. Fcap. 8vo., price 2s. 6d. cloth, 3s. gilt edges.

Pictures of Girl Life.

By CATHARINE AUGUSTA HOWELL, author of "Pages of Child Life." Frontispiece by F. ELLZE. Fcap. 3vo., price 3s. 6d. cloth, 4s. gilt edges.

The Four Seasons.

A Short Account of the Structure of Plants, founded on a Series of Lectures prepared for the Working Men's Institute, Paris.

(*Nearly ready.*)

Nursery Nonsense;

Or Rhymes without Reason, by D'ARCY W. THOMPSON, with sixty Illustrations, by C. H. BENNETT. Second edition. Imperial 16mo., price 2s. 6d. cloth; or 4s. 6d. coloured, cloth elegant, gilt edges.

" The funniest book we have seen for an age, and quite as harmless as hearty."—*Daily Review.*

" Whatever Mr. Bennett does, has some touch in it of a true genius."—*Examiner.*

Spectropia;

Or, Surprising Spectral Illusions, showing Ghosts everywhere and of any Colour. By J. H. BROWN. Third edition. Quarto. Price, 2s. 6d. fancy boards.

" One of the best scientific toy books we have seen."—*Athenæum.*

"A clever book. The illusions are founded on true scientific principles."—*Chemical News.*

" We heartily commend Mr. Brown's ingenious work."—*The Lancet.*

BY THE AUTHOR OF ' MARYPOWELL,' ETC.

The Interrupted Wedding;

A Hungarian Tale. With Frontispiece, by HENRY WARREN. Post 8vo., price 6s. cloth.

" The author treads on fresh ground, and introduces us to a people of whose home scenes we are glad to read such truthful natural descriptions."—*Athenæum.*

" The story is excellently told, as might be expected from the peculiar powers of the narrator."—*Saturday Review.*

NEW BOYS' BOOK BY MRS. HENRY WOOD.

William Allair;

Or, Running away to Sea, by Mrs. H. WOOD, author of " East Lynne, " The Channings," etc. Frontispiece by F. GILBERT. Fcap. 8vo., price 2s. 6d., cloth, 3s. gilt edges.

" There is a fascination about Mrs. Wood's writings, from which neither old nor young can escape."—*Bell's Messenger.*

The Happy Home;

Or the Children at the Red House, by LADY LUSHINGTON. Illustrated by G. J. PINWELL. Super royal 16mo., price 3s. 6d. cloth, 4s. 6d. coloured, gilt edges.

" A happy mixture of fact and fiction. Altogether it is one of the best books of the kind we have met with."—*Guardian.*

Our Birth Days;

And how to improve them, by Mrs. E. DAVENPORT, author of "Fickle Flora," etc. Frontispiece by D. H. FRISTON. Fcap. 8vo., price 2s. 6d. cloth, 3s. gilt edges.

"Most admirably suited as a gift to young girls."—*British Mother's Magazine.*

Historical Tales of Lancastrian Times.

By the Rev. H. P. DUNSTER, M.A., with illustrations by JOHN FRANKLIN. Fcap. 8vo., price 5s. cloth, 5s. 6d. gilt edges.

"A volume skilfully treated."—*Saturday Review.*

"Conveys a good deal of information about the manners and customs of England and France in the 15th Century."—*Gentlemen's Magazine.*

Tiny Stories for Tiny Readers in Tiny Words.

By the author of "Tuppy," "Triumphs of Steam," &c., with Twelve Illustrations, by HARRISON WEIR. Second edition. Super Royal 16mo., price 2s. 6d. cloth, 4s. 6d. coloured, cloth, elegant gilt edges.

Little by Little.

A series of Graduated Lessons in the Art of Reading Music, by the author of "Conversations on Harmony." Oblong 8vo., price 3s. 6d. cloth.

"One of the best productions of the kind which have yet appeared."—*Charles Steggall. Mus. D., Cantab.*

Memorable Battles in English History.

Where Fought, why Fought, and their Results. With Lives of the Commanders. By W. H. DAVENPORT ADAMS, author of "Neptune's Heroes; or, the Sea-kings of England." Frontispiece by ROBERT DUDLEY. Post 8vo. price 7s. 6d. extra cloth.

"Of the care and honesty of the author's labours, the book gives abundant proof."—*Athenæum.*

Our Soldiers;

Or, Anecdotes of the Campaigns and Gallant Deeds of the British Army during the reign of Her Majesty Queen Victoria. By W. H. G. KINGSTON. With Frontispiece from a Painting in the Victoria Cross Gallery. Fcp. 8vo. price 3s. cloth; 3s. 6d. gilt edges.

Our Sailors;

Or, Anecdotes of the Engagements and Gallant Deeds of the British Navy during the reign of Her Majesty Queen Victoria. By W. H. G. KINGSTON. With Frontispiece. Fcap. 8vo. price 3s. cloth; 3s. 6d. gilt edges.

"These volumes abundantly prove that both our officers and men in the Army and Navy, have been found as ready as ever to dare, and to do as was dared and done of yore, when led by a Nelson or a Wellington."

The Loves of Tom Tucker and Little Bo-Peep.

Written and Illustrated by THOMAS HOOD. Quarto, price 2s. 6d. coloured plates.

" Full of fun and of good innocent humour. The Illustrations are excellent."—The Critic.

Scenes and Stories of the Rhine.

By M. BETHAM EDWARDS, author of " Holidays among the Mountains," etc. With Illustrations by F. W. KEYL. Super Royal 16mo. price 3s. 6d. cloth; 4s. 6d. coloured, gilt edges.

" Full of amusing incidents, good stories, and sprightly pictures."—The Dial.

Holidays Among the Mountains;

Or, Scenes and Stories of Wales. By M. BETHAM EDWARDS. Illustrated by F. J. SKILL. Super royal 16mo.; price 3s. 6d. cloth; 4s. 6d. coloured, gilt edges.

Nursery Fun;

Or, the Little Folks' Picture Book. The Illustrations by C. H. BENNETT. Quarto, price 2s. 6d. coloured plates.

" Will be greeted with shouts of laughter in any nursery."—The Critic.

Play-Room Stories;

Or, How to make Peace. By GEORGIANA M. CRAIK. With Illustrations by C. GREEN. Super Royal 16mo. price 3s. 6d. cloth; 4s. 6d. coloured, gilt edges.

" This Book will come with ' peace' upon its wings into many a crowded playroom." —Art Journal.

Fickle Flora,

and her Sea Side Friends. By EMMA DAVENPORT, author of " Live Toys," etc. With Illustrations by J. Absolon. Super Royal 16mo. price 3s. 6d. cloth; 4s. 6d. coloured, gilt edges.

Live Toys;

Or, Anecdotes of our Four-legged and other Pets. By EMMA DAVENPORT. With Illustrations by HARRISON WEIR. Second Edition. Super Royal 16mo. price 2s. 6d. cloth; 3s. 6d. coloured, gilt edges.

" One of the best kind of books for youthful reading."—Guardian.

The Faithful Hound.

A Story in Verse, founded on fact. By LADY THOMAS. With Illustrations by H. WEIR. Imperial 16mo, price 2s. 6d. cloth; 3s. 6d. coloured, gilt edges.

DEDICATED BY PERMISSION TO ALFRED TENNYSON.

The Story of King Arthur,

and his Knights of the Round Table. With Six Beautiful Illustrations, by G. H. Thomas. Post 8vo. price 7s. cloth; 9s. coloured, gilt edges.

"Heartily glad are we to welcome the glorious old tale in its present shape."—*Gentleman's Magazine.*

ALFRED ELWES' BOOKS FOR BOYS.

With Illustrations, Fcap. 8vo. price 5s. each cloth; 5s. 6d. gilt edges.

Luke Ashleigh;

Or, School Life in Holland. Illustrated by G. Du Maurier.

" The author's best book, by a writer whose popularity with boys is great."—*Athenæum.*

Guy Rivers;

Or, a Boy's Struggles in the Great World. Illustrations by H. Anelay.

"Mr. Elwes sustains his reputation. The moral tone is excellent, and boys will derive from it both pleasure and profit."—*Athenæum.*

Ralph Seabrooke;

Or, The Adventures of a Young Artist in Piedmont and Tuscany. Illustrated by Dudley.

Frank and Andrea;

Or Forest Life in the Island of Sardinia. Illustrated by Dudley.

" The descriptions of Sardinian life and scenery are admirable."—*Athenæum.*

Paul Blake;

Or, the Story of a Boy's Perils in the Islands of Corsica and Monte Cristo. Illustrated by H. Anelay.

" This spirited and engaging story will lead our young friends to a very intimate acquaintance with the island of Corsica."—*Art Journal.*

CAPTAIN MARRYAT'S DAUGHTER.

Harry at School;

By Emilia Marryat. With Illustrations by Absolon. Super Royal 16mo. price 2s. 6d. cloth; 3s. 6d. coloured, gilt edges.

"Really good, and fitted to delight little boys."—*Spectator.*

Long Evenings;

Or, Stories for My Little Friends, by Emilia Marryat. Illustrated by Absolon. Second Edition. Price 2s. 6d. cloth; 3s. 6d. coloured, gilt edges.

"Let Papas and Mammas, making choice of Christmas Gift Books, ask for this."—*Athenæum.*

THOMAS HOOD'S DAUGHTER.

My Grandmother's Budget

of Stories and Verses. By FRANCES FREELING BRODERIP. Illustrated by her brother, THOMAS HOOD. Price 3s. 6d. cloth; 4s. 6d. coloured, gilt edges.

"Some of the most charming little inventions that ever adorned the department of literature."—*Illustrated Times.*

Tiny Tadpole;

And other Tales. By FRANCES FREELING BRODERIP, daughter of the late Thomas Hood. With Illustrations by HER BROTHER. Super-Royal 16mo. price 3s. 6d. cloth; 4s. 6d. coloured, gilt edges.

"A remarkable book, by the brother and sister of a family in which genius and fun are inherited."—*Saturday Review.*

Funny Fables for Little Folks.

By FRANCES FREELING BRODERIP. Illustrated by her Brother. Super Royal 16mo. price 2s. 6d. cloth; 3s. 6d. coloured, gilt edges.

"The Fables contain the happiest mingling of fun, fancy, humour, and instruction."—*Art Journal.*

———

Jack Frost and Betty Snow;

With other Tales for Wintry Nights and Rainy Days. Illustrated by H. Weir. 2s. 6d. cloth; 3s. 6d. coloured, gilt edges.

"The dedication of these pretty tales, prove by whom they are written; they are indelibly stamped with that natural and graceful method of amusing while instructing, which only persons of genius possess."—*Art Journal.*

WILLIAM DALTON'S BOOKS FOR BOYS.

With Illustrations; Fcap. 8vo. price 5s. each cloth; 5s. 6d. gilt edges.

Lost in Ceylon;

The Story of a Boy and Girl's Adventures in the Woods and Wilds of the Lion King of Kandy. Illustrated by WEIR.

"Clever, exciting and full of true descriptions of the creatures and sights in that noble island."—*Literary Gazette.*

The White Elephant;

Or the Hunters of Ava, and the King of the Golden Foot. Illustrated by WEIR.

"Full of dash, nerve and spirit, and withal freshness."—*Literary Gazette.*

The War Tiger;

Or, The Adventures and Wonderful Fortunes of the Young Sea-Chief and his Lad Chow. Illustrated by H. S. MELVILLE.

"A tale of lively adventure vigorously told, and embodying much curious information." *Illustrated News.*

The Boy's own Toy Maker.

A Practical Illustrated Guide to the useful employment of Leisure Hours. By E. LANDELLS. With Two Hundred Cuts. Sixth Edition. Royal 16mo, price 2s. 6d., cloth.

" A new and valuable form of endless amusement."—*Nonconformist.*
" We recommend it to all who have children to be instructed and amused."—*Economist.*

The Girl's Own Toy Maker,

And Book of Recreation. By E. and A. LANDELLS. Third Edition. With 200 Illustrations. Royal 16mo. price 2s. 6d. cloth.

" A perfect magazine of information."—*Illustrated News of the World.*

Home Pastime;

Or, The Child's Own Toy Maker. With practical instructions. By E. LANDELLS. New and Cheaper Edition, price 3s. 6d. complete, with the Cards, and Descriptive Letterpress.

⁎ By this novel and ingenious "Pastime," Twelve beautiful Models can be made by Children from the Cards, by attending to the Plain and Simple Instructions in the Book.

" As a delightful exercise of ingenuity, and a most sensible mode of passing a winter's evening, we commend the Child's own Toy Maker."—*Illustrated News.*
" Should be in every house blessed with the presence of children."—*The Field.*

The Illustrated Paper Model Maker;

Containing Twelve Pictorial Subjects, with Descriptive Letter-press and Diagrams for the construction of the Models. By E. LANDELLS. Price 2s. in a neat Envelope.

" A most excellent mode of educating both eye and hand in the knowledge of form."—*English Churchman.*

Fairy Land;

Or, Recreation for the Rising Generation, in Prose and Verse. By THOMAS and JANE HOOD. Illustrated by T. HOOD, Jun. Super royal 16mo; price 3s. 6d. cloth; 4s. 6d. coloured gilt edges.

" These tales are charming. Before it goes into the Nursery, we recommend all grown up people should study ' Fairy Land'—*Blackwood.*'"

The Headlong Career and Woful Ending of Precocious PIGGY.

Written for his Children, by the late THOMAS HOOD. With a Preface by his Daughter; and Illustrated by his Son. Third Edition. Post 4to, fancy boards, price 2s. 6d., coloured.

" The Illustrations are intensely humourous."—*The Critic.*

BY THE AUTHOR OF "TRIUMPHS OF STEAM," ETC.

Meadow Lea;

Or, the Gipsy Children; a Story founded on fact. By the Author of
" The Triumphs of Steam," " Our Eastern Empire," etc. With Illustrations by JOHN GILBERT. Fcap. 8vo. price 4s. 6d. cloth; 5s. gilt edges.

The Triumphs of Steam;

Or, Stories from the Lives of Watt, Arkwright, and Stephenson. With
Illustrations by J. GILBERT. Dedicated by permission to Robert
Stephenson, Esq., M.P. Second edition. Royal 16mo, price 3s. 6d.
cloth; 4s. 6d., coloured, gilt edges.

" A most delicious volume of examples."--*Art Journal.*

Our Eastern Empire;

Or, Stories from the History of British India. Second Edition, with
Continuation to the Proclamation of Queen Victoria. With Four
Illustrations. Royal 16mo. cloth 3s. 6d.; 4s. 6d. coloured, gilt edges.

" These stories are charming, and convey a general view of the progress of our Empire in
the East. The tales are told with admirable clearness."—*Athenæum.*

Might not Right;

Or, Stories of the Discovery and Conquest of America. Illustrated by J. Gilbert. Royal 16mo. price 3s. 6d. cloth; 4s. 6d.
coloured, gilt edges.

" With the fortunes of Columbus, Cortes, and Pizarro, for the staple of these stories, the
writer has succeeded in producing a very interesting volume."—*Illustrated News.*

Tuppy;

Or the Autobiography of a Donkey. By the Author of " The Triumphs
of Steam," etc., etc. Illustrated by HARRISON WEIR. Super Royal
16mo. price 2s. 6d. cloth; 3s. 6d. coloured, gilt edges.

" A very intelligent donkey, worthy of the distinction conferred upon him by the artist."
—*Art Journal.*

---

1. The History of a Quartern Loaf.

in Rhymes and Pictures. By WILLIAM NEWMAN. 12 Illustrations.
Price 6d. plain, 1s. coloured. 2s. 6d. on linen, and bound in cloth.

Uniform in size and price,

2. The History of a Cup of Tea.

3. The History of a Scuttle of Coals.

4. The History of a Lump of Sugar.

5. The History of a Bale of Cotton.

6. The History of a Golden Sovereign.

*** Nos. 1 to 3 and 4 to 6, may be had bound in Two Volumes. Cloth,
price 2s. each, plain; 3s. 6d. coloured.

Distant Homes;

Or, the Graham Family in New Zealand. By Mrs. I. E. Aylmer. With Illustrations by J. Jackson. Super Royal 16mo. price 3s. 6d. cloth; 4s. 6d. coloured, gilt edges.

" English children will be delighted with the history of the Graham Family, and be enabled to form pleasant and truthful conceptions of the ' Distant Homes' inhabited by their kindred."—*Athenæum.*

Neptune's Heroes : or The Sea Kings of England;

from Hawkins to Franklin. By W. H. Davenport Adams. Illustrated by Morgan. Fcap. 8vo; price 5s. cloth; 5s. 6d. gilt edges.

"We trust Old England may ever have writers as ready and able to interpret to her children the noble lives of her greatest men."—*Athenæum.*

Hand Shadows,

To be thrown upon the Wall. By Henry Bursill. First and Second Series each containing Eighteen Original Designs. 4to price 2s. each plain; 2s. 6d. coloured.

" Uncommonly clever—some wonderful effects are produced."—*The Press.*

WORKS FOR DISTRIBUTION.

A Woman's Secret;

Or How to Make Home Happy. 26th Thousand. 18mo. price 6d.

By the same Author, uniform in size and price,

Woman's Work; or, How she can Help the Sick.
15th Thousand.

A Chapter of Accidents;

Or, the Mother's Assistant in cases of Burns, Scalds, Cuts, &c. 7th Thousand.

Pay To-day, Trust To-morrow;

A Story illustrative of the Evils of the Tally System. 6th Thousand.

Nursery Work;

Or Hannah Baker's First Place. 4th Thousand.

Family Prayers for Cottage Homes;

With a Few Words on Prayer, and Select Scripture Passages. Fcap. 8vo. price 4d. limp cloth.

*** These little works are admirably adapted for circulation among the working classes.

W. H. G. KINGSTON'S BOOKS FOR BOYS.

With Illustrations. Fcap. 8vo. price 5s. each, cloth; 5s. 6d. gilt edges.

True Blue;

Or, the Life and Adventures of a British Seaman of the Old School.

"There is about all Mr. Kingston's tales a spirit of hopefulness, honesty, and cheery good principle, which makes them most wholesome, as well as most interesting reading."—*Era.*

Will Weatherhelm;

Or, the Yarn of an Old Sailor about his Early Life and Adventures.

"We tried the story on an audience of boys, who one and all declared it to be capital."—*Athenæum.*

Fred Markham in Russia;

Or, the Boy Travellers in the Land of the Czar.

"Most admirably does this book unite a capital narrative, with the communication of valuable information respecting Russia."—*Nonconformist.*

Salt Water;

Or Neil D'Arcy's Sea Life and Adventures. With Eight Illustrations.

"With the exception of Capt. Marryat, we know of no English author who will compare with Mr. Kingston as a writer of books of nautical adventure."—*Illustrated News.*

Manco, the Peruvian Chief;

With Illustrations by CARL SCHMOLZE.

"A capital book; the story being one of much interest, and presenting a good account of the history and institutions, the customs and manners, of the country."—*Literary Gazette.*

Mark Seaworth;

A Tale of the Indian Ocean. By the Author of "Peter the Whaler," etc. With Illustrations by J. ABSOLON. Second Edition.

"No more interesting, nor more safe book, can be put into the hands of youth; and to boys especially, 'Mark Seaworth' will be a treasure of delight."—*Art Journal.*

Peter the Whaler;

His early Life and Adventures in the Arctic Regions. Third Edition. Illustrations by E. DUNCAN.

"A better present for a boy of an active turn of mind could not be found. The tone of the book is manly, healthful, and vigorous."—*Weekly News.*

"A book which the old may, but which the young must, read when they have once begun it."—*Athenæum.*

Old Nurse's Book of Rhymes, Jingles, and Dittics.

Illustrated by C. H. BENNETT. With Ninety Engravings. New Edition. Fcap. 4to., price 3s. 6d. cloth, plain, or 6s. coloured.

"The illustrations are all so replete with fun and imagination, that we scarcely know who will be most pleased with the book, the good-natured grandfather who gives it, or the chubby grandchild who gets it, for a Christmas-Box."—*Notes and Queries.*

Home Amusements.

A Choice Collection of Riddles, Charades, Conundrums, Parlour Games, and Forfeits. By PETER PUZZLEWELL, Esq., of Rebus Hall. New Edition, with Frontispiece by PHIZ. 16mo, 2s. 6d. cloth.

Clara Hope;

Or, the Blade and the Ear. By MISS MILNER. With Frontispiece by Birket Foster. Fcap. 8vo. price 3s. 6d. cloth; 4s. 6d. cloth elegant, gilt edges.

"A beautiful narrative, showing how bad habits may be eradicated, and evil tempers subdued."—*British Mother's Journal.*

The Adventures and Experiences of Biddy Dork-

ING and of the FAT FROG. Edited by MRS. S. C. HALL. Illustrated by H. Weir. 2s. 6d. cloth; 3s. 6d. coloured, gilt edges.

"Most amusingly and wittily told."—*Morning Herald.*

Historical Acting Charades;

Or, Amusements for Winter Evenings, by the author of "Cat and Dog," etc. New Edition. Fcap. 8vo., price 3s. 6d. cloth; 4s. gilt edges.

"A rare book for Christmas parties, and of practical value."—*Illustrated News.*

The Story of Jack and the Giants:

With thirty-five Illustrations by RICHARD DOYLE. Beautifully printed. New and Cheaper Edition. Fcap. 4to. price 2s. 6d. cloth; 3s. 6d. coloured, extra cloth, gilt edges.

"In Doyle's drawings we have wonderful conceptions, which will secure the book a place amongst the treasures of collectors, as well as excite the imaginations of children."—*Illustrated Times.*

Granny's Wonderful Chair;

And its Tales of Fairy Times. By FRANCES BROWNE. Illustrations by KENNY MEADOWS. 3s. 6d. cloth, 4s. 6d. coloured.

"One of the happiest blendings of marvel and moral we have ever seen."—*Literary Gazette.*

The Early Dawn;

Or, Stories to Think about. Illustrated by H. WEIR, etc. Small 4to.; price 2s. 6d. cloth; 3s. 6d. coloured, gilt edges.

"The matter is both wholesome and instructive, and must fascinate as well as benefit the young."—*Literarium.*

Angelo;

Or, the Pine Forest among the Alps. By GERALDINE E. JEWSBURY, author of "The Adopted Child," etc. With Illustrations by JOHN ABSOLON. Small 4to; price 2s. 6d. cloth; 3s. 6d. coloured, gilt edges.

"As pretty a child's story as one might look for on a winter's day."—*Examiner.*

Tales of Magic and Meaning.

Written and Illustrated by ALFRED CROWQUILL. Small 4to.; price 3s. 6d. cloth; 4s. 6d. coloured.

"Cleverly written, abounding in frolic and pathos, and inculcates so pure a moral, that we must pronounce him a very fortunate little fellow, who catches these 'Tales of Magic,' as a windfall from 'The Christmas Tree'."—*Athenæum.*

Faggots for the Fire Side;

Or, Tales of Fact and Fancy. By PETER PARLEY. With Twelve Tinted Illustrations. New Edition. Foolscap 8vo.; 3s. 6d., cloth; 4s. 6d. coloured, gilt edges.

"A new book by Peter Parley is a pleasant greeting for all boys and girls, wherever the English language is spoken and read. He has a happy method of conveying information, while seeming to address himself to the imagination."—*The Critic.*

Letters from Sarawak,

Addressed to a Child; embracing an Account of the Manners, Customs, and Religion of the Inhabitants of Borneo, with Incidents of Missionary Life among the Natives. By Mrs. M'DOUGALL. Fourth Thousand, with Illustrations. 3s. 6d. cloth.

All is new, interesting, and admirably told."—*Church and State Gazette.*

The Discontented Children;

And How they were Cured. By MARY and ELIZABETH KIRBY. Illustrated by H. K. BROWNE (Phiz.). Second edition, price 2s. 6d. cloth; 3s. 6d. coloured, gilt edges.

"We know no better method of banishing 'discontent' from school-room and nursery than by introducing this wise and clever story to their inmates."—Art Journal.

The Talking Bird;

Or, the Little Girl who knew what was going to happen. By M. and E. KIRBY. With Illustrations by H. K. BROWNE (PHIZ). Small 4to. Price 2s. 6d. cloth; 3s. 6d. coloured, gilt edges.

"The story is ingeniously told, and the moral clearly shown."—Athenæum.

Julia Maitland;

Or, Pride goes before a Fall. By M. and E. KIRBY. Illustrated by ABSOLON. Price 2s. 6d. cloth; 3s. 6d. coloured, gilt edges.

"It is nearly such a story as Miss Edgeworth might have written on the same theme."— The Press.

COMICAL PICTURE BOOKS.

Uniform in size with "The Struwwelpeter."

Each with Sixteen large Coloured Plates, price 2s. 6d., in fancy boards, or mounted on cloth, 1s. extra.

Picture Fables.

Written and Illustrated by ALFRED CROWQUILL.

The Careless Chicken;

By the BARON KRAKEMSIDES. By ALFRED CROWQUILL.

Funny Leaves for the Younger Branches.

By the BARON KRAKEMSIDES, of Burstenoudelafen Castle. Illustrated by ALFRED CROWQUILL.

Laugh and Grow Wise;

By the Senior Owl of Ivy Hall. With Sixteen large coloured Plates. Price 2s. 6d. fancy boards; or 3s. 6d. mounted on cloth.

The Remarkable History of the House that Jack

Built. Splendidly Illustrated and magnificently Illuminated by THE SON OF A GENIUS. Price 2s. *in fancy cover.*

"Magnificent in suggestion, and most comical in expression!"—*Athenæum.*

A Peep at the Pixies;

Or, Legends of the West. By Mrs. BRAY. Author of "Life of Stothard," "Trelawny," etc., etc. With Illustrations by Phiz. Superroyal 16mo, price 3s. 6d. cloth; 4s. 6d. coloured, gilt edges.

"A peep at the actual Pixies of Devonshire, faithfully described by Mrs. Bray, is a treat. Her knowledge of the locality, her affection for her subject, her exquisite feeling for nature, and her real delight in fairy lore, have given a freshness to the little volume we did not expect. The notes at the end contain matter of interest for all who feel a desire to know the origin of such tales and legends."—*Art Journal.*

A BOOK FOR EVERY CHILD.

The Favourite Picture Book;

A Gallery of Delights, designed for the Amusement and Instruction of the Young. With several Hundred Illustrations from Drawings by J. ABSOLON, H. K. BROWNE (Phiz), J. GILBERT, T. LANDSEER, J. LEECH, J. S. PROUT, H. WEIR, etc. New Edition. Royal 4to., price 3s. 6d., bound in a new and Elegant Cover; 7s. 6d. coloured; 10s. 6d. mounted on cloth and coloured.

Ocean and her Rulers;

A Narrative of the Nations who have held dominion over the Sea; and comprising a brief History of Navigation. By ALFRED ELWES. With Frontispiece. Fcap. 8vo, 5s. cloth; 5s. 6d. gilt edges.

"The volume is replete with valuable and interesting information; and we cordially recommend it as a useful auxiliary in the school-room, and entertaining companion in the library."—*Morning Post.*

Berries and Blossoms.

A Verse Book for Children. By T. WESTWOOD. With Title and Frontispiece printed in Colours. Imperial 16mo, price 3s. 6d. cloth, gilt edges.

Sunday Evenings with Sophia;

Or, Little Talks on Great Subjects. A Book for Girls. By LEONORA G. BELL. Frontispiece by J. ABSOLON. Fcap. 8vo, price 2s. 6d. cloth.

" A very suitable gift for a thoughtful girl."—*Bell's Messenger.*

The Wonders of Home, in Eleven Stories.

By GRANDFATHER GREY. With Illustrations. Third and Cheaper Edition. Royal 16mo., 2s. 6d. cloth; 3s. 6d. coloured, gilt edges.

CONTENTS.—1. The Story of a Cup of Tea.—2. A Lump of Coal.—3. Some Hot Water.—4. A Piece of Sugar.—5. The Milk Jug.—6. A Pin.—7. Jenny's Sash.—8. Harry's Jacket.—9. A Tumbler.—10. A Knife.—11. This Book.

" The idea is excellent, and its execution equally commendable. The subjects are well selected, and are very happily told in a light yet sensible manner."—*Weekly News.*

Cat and Dog;

Or, Memoirs of Puss and the Captain. Illustrated by WEIR. Seventh Edition. Super-royal 16mo, 2s. 6d. cloth; 3s. 6d. coloured, gilt edges.

" The author of this amusing little tale is, evidently, a keen observer of nature. The illustrations are well executed; and the moral, which points the tale, is conveyed in the most attractive form."—*Britannia.*

The Doll and Her Friends;

Or, Memoirs of the Lady Seraphina. By the Author of " Cat and Dog." Third Edition. With Four Illustrations by H. K. BROWNE (Phiz). 2s. 6d., cloth; 3s. 6d. coloured, gilt edges.

"Evidently written by one who has brought great powers to bear upon a small matter."—*Morning Herald.*

Tales from Catland;

Dedicated to the Young Kittens of England. By an OLD TABBY. Illustrated by H. WEIR. Fourth Edition. Small 4to, 2s. 6d. plain; 3s. 6d. coloured, gilt edges.

" The combination of quiet humour and sound sense has made this one of the pleasantest little books of the season."—*Lady's Newspaper.*

Blind Man's Holiday;

Or Short Tales for the Nursery. By the Author of " Mia and Charlie," " Sidney Grey," etc. Illustrated by John Absolon. Super Royal 16mo. price 3s. 6d. cloth; 4s. 6d. coloured, gilt edges.

" Very true to nature and admirable in feeling."—*Guardian.*

Scenes of Animal Life and Character.

From Nature and Recollection. In Twenty Plates. By J. B. 4to, price 2s., plain; 2s. 6d., coloured, fancy boards.

" Truer, heartier, more playful, or more enjoyable sketches of animal life could scarcely be found anywhere."—*Spectator.*

Anecdotes of the Habits and Instincts of Animals.

Third and Cheaper Edition. With Illustrations by HARRISON WEIR.
Fcap. 8vo, 3s. 6d. cloth; 4s. gilt edges.

Anecdotes of the Habits and Instincts of Birds,

REPTILES, and FISHES. With Illustrations by HARRISON WEIR.
Second and Cheaper Edition. Fcap. 8vo, 3s. 6d. cloth; 4s. gilt edges.

" Amusing, instructive, and ably written."—*Literary Gazette.*
" Mrs. Lee's authorities—to name only one, Professor Owen—are, for the most part first-rate.'—*Athenæum.*

Twelve Stories of the Sayings and Doings of

ANIMALS. With Illustrations by J. W. ARCHER. Third Edition.
Super-royal 16mo, 2s. 6d. cloth; 3s. 6d. coloured, gilt edges.

" It is just such books as this that educate the imagination of children, and enlist their sympathies for the brute creation."—*Nonconformist.*

Familiar Natural History.

With Forty-two Illustrations from Original Drawings by HARRISON
WEIR. Super-royal 16mo, 3s. 6d. cloth; 5s. coloured gilt edges.

Playing at Settlers;

Or, the Faggot House. Illustrated by GILBERT. Second Edition.
Price 2s. 6d. cloth; 3s. 6d. coloured, gilt edges.

Adventures in Australia;

Or, the Wanderings of Captain Spencer in the Bush and the Wilds.
Second Edition. Illustrated by PROUT. Fcap. 8vo., 5s. cloth; 5s. 6d.
gilt edges.

" This volume should find a place in every school library ; and it will, we are sure, be a very welcome and useful prize."—*Educational Times.*

The African Wanderers; .

Or, the Adventures of Carlos and Antonio; embracing interesting
Descriptions of the Manners and Customs of the Western Tribes, and
the Natural Productions of the Country. Third Edition. With Eight
Engravings. Fcap. 8vo, 5s. cloth; 5s. 6d. gilt edges.

" For fascinating adventure, and rapid succession of incident, the volume is equal to any relation of travel we ever read."—*Britannia.*
" In strongly recommending this admirable work to the attention of young readers, we feel that we are rendering a real service to the cause of African civilization."—*Patriot.*

Sir Thomas; or, the Adventures of a Cornish

BARONET IN WESTERN AFRICA. With Illustrations by
J. GILBERT. Fcap. 8vo.; 3s. 6d. cloth.

Harry Hawkins's H-Book;

Shewing how he learned to aspirate his H's. Frontispiece by H. WEIR. Second Edition. Super-royal 16mo, price 6d.

" No family or school-room within, or indeed beyond, the sound of Bow bells, should be without this merry manual."—*Art Journal.*

The Family Bible Newly Opened;

With Uncle Goodwin's account of it. By JEFFERYS TAYLOR. Frontispiece by J. GILBERT. Fcap. 8vo, 3s. 6d. cloth.

" A very good account of the Sacred Writings, adapted to the tastes, feelings, and intelligence of young people."—*Educational Times.*

Kate and Rosalind;

Or, Early Experiences. By the author of " Quicksands on Foreign Shores," etc. Fcap. 8vo, 3s. 6d. cloth; 4s. gilt edges.

" A book of unusual merit. The story is exceedingly well told, and the characters are drawn with a freedom and boldness seldom met with."—*Church of England Quarterly.*

" We have not room to exemplify the skill with which Puseyism is tracked and detected. The Irish scenes are of an excellence that has not been surpassed since the best days of Miss Edgeworth."—*Fraser's Magazine.*

Good in Everything;

Or, The Early History of Gilbert Harland. By Mrs. BARWELL, Author of " Little Lessons for Little Learners," etc. Second Edition. With Illustrations by JOHN GILBERT. Royal 16mo., 2s. 6d. cloth; 3s. 6d., coloured, gilt edges.

" The moral of this exquisite little tale will do more good than a thousand set tasks abounding with dry and uninteresting truisms."—*Bell's Messenger.*

The Fairy Tales of Science.

A Book for Youth. By J. C. BROUGH. With 16 Beautiful Illustrations by C. H. BENNETT. Fcap. 8vo, price 5s., cloth; 5s. 6d. gilt edges.
" Science, perhaps, was never made more attractive and easy of entrance into the youthful mind."—*The Builder.*
" Altogether the volume is one of the most original, as well as one of the most useful, books of the season."—*Gentleman's Magazine.*

ELEGANT GIFT FOR A LADY.

Trees, Plants, and Flowers;

Their Beauties, Uses and Influences. By Mrs. R. LEE, Author of "The African Wanderers," etc. With beautiful coloured Illustrations by J. ANDREWS. 8vo, price 10s. 6d., cloth elegant, gilt edges.

"The volume is at once useful as a botanical work, and exquisite as the ornament of a boudoir table."—*Britannia.* "As full of interest as of beauty."—*Art Journal.*

NEW AND BEAUTIFUL LIBRARY EDITION.

The Vicar of Wakefield;

A Tale. By OLIVER GOLDSMITH. Printed by Whittingham. With Eight Illustrations by J. ABSOLON. Square fcap. 8vo, price 5s., cloth; 7s. half-bound morocco, Roxburghe style; 10s. 6d. antique morocco.

Mr. Absolon's graphic sketches add greatly to the interest of the volume: altogether, it is as pretty an edition of the 'Vicar' as we have seen. Mrs. Primrose herself would consider it 'well dressed.'"—*Art Journal.*

"A delightful edition of one of the most delightful of works: the fine old type and thick paper make this volume attractive to any lover of books."—*Edinburgh Guardian.*

WORKS BY MRS. LOUDON.

Domestic Pets;

Their Habits and Management; with Illustrative Anecdotes. By MRS. LOUDON. With Engravings from Drawings by HARRISON WEIR. Second Thousand. Fcap. 8vo, 2s. 6d. cloth.

CONTENTS:—The Dog, Cat, Squirrel, Rabbit, Guinea-Pig, White Mice, the Parrot and other Talking Birds, Singing Birds, Doves and Pigeons, Gold and Silver Fish.

"A most attractive and instructive little work. All who study Mrs. Loudon's pages will be able to treat their pets with certainty and wisdom."—*Standard of Freedom.*

Glimpses of Nature;

And Objects of Interest described during a Visit to the Isle of Wight. Designed to assist and encourage Young Persons in forming habits of observation. By Mrs. LOUDON. Second Edition, enlarged. With Forty-one Illustrations. 3s. 6d. cloth.

"We could not recommend a more valuable little volume. It is full of information, conveyed in the most agreeable manner."—*Literary Gazette.*

Tales of School Life.

By AGNES LOUDON, Author of "Tales for Young People." With Illustrations by JOHN ABSOLON. Second Edition. Royal 16mo, 2s. 6d. plain; 3s. 6d. coloured, gilt edges.

"These reminiscences of school days will be recognised as truthful pictures of every-day occurrence. The style is colloquial and pleasant, and therefore well suited to those for whose perusal it is intended."—*Athenæum.*

Clarissa Donnelly;

Or, The History of an Adopted Child. By GERALDINE E. JEWSBURY. With an Illustration by JOHN ABSOLON. Fcap. 8vo, 3s. 6d. cloth; 4s. gilt edges.

"With wonderful power, only to be matched by as admirable a simplicity, Miss Jewsbury has narrated the history of a child. For nobility of purpose, for simple, nervous writing, and for artistic construction, it is one of the most valuable works of the day."—*Lady's Companion.*

The Day of a Baby Boy;

A Story for a Young Child. By E. BERGER. With Illustrations by JOHN ABSOLON. Third Edition. Super-royal 16mo, price 2s. 6d. cloth; 3s. 6d. coloured, gilt edges.

"A sweet little book for the nursery."—*Christian Times.*

Every-Day Things;

Or, Useful Knowledge respecting the principal Animal, Vegetable, and Mineral Substances in common use. Written for Young Persons. Second Edition, revised. 18mo., 1s. 6d. cloth.

"A little encyclopædia of useful knowledge, deserving a place in every juvenile library." —*Evangelical Magazine.*

PRICE SIXPENCE EACH, PLAIN; ONE SHILLING, COLOURED

In Super-Royal 16mo., beautifully printed, each with Seven Illustrations by HARRISON WEIR, *and Descriptions by* MRS. LEE.

1. BRITISH ANIMALS. First Series.
2. BRITISH ANIMALS. Second Series.
3. BRITISH BIRDS.
4. FOREIGN ANIMALS. First Series.
5. FOREIGN ANIMALS. Second Series.
6. FOREIGN BIRDS.

⁎ Or bound in One Volume under the title of "Familiar Natural History," *see page* 17.

Uniform in size and price with the above.

THE FARM AND ITS SCENES. With Six Pictures from Drawings by HARRISON WEIR.

THE DIVERTING HISTORY OF JOHN GILPIN. With Six Illustrations by WATTS PHILLIPS.

THE PEACOCK AT HOME, AND BUTTERFLY'S BALL. With Four Illustrations by HARRISON WEIR.

WORKS BY THE AUTHOR OF MAMMA'S BIBLE STORIES.

Fanny and her Mamma;

Or, Easy Lessons for Children. In which it is attempted to bring Scriptural Principles into daily practice. Illustrated by J. GILBERT. Third Edition. 16mo, 2s. 6d. cloth; 3s. 6d. coloured, gilt edges.

"A little book in beautiful large clear type, to suit the capacity of infant readers, which we can with pleasure recommend."—*Christian Ladies' Magazine.*

Short and Simple Prayers,

For the Use of Young Children. With Hymns. Fifth Edition. Square 16mo, 1s. 6d. cloth.

"Well adapted to the capacities of children—beginning with the simplest forms which the youngest child may lisp at its mother's knee, and proceeding with those suited to its gradually advancing age. Special prayers, designed for particular circumstances and occasions, are added. We cordially recommend the book."—*Christian Guardian.*

Mamma's Bible Stories,

For her Little Boys and Girls, adapted to the capacities of very young Children. Eleventh Edition, with Twelve Engravings. 2s. 6d. cloth; 3s. 6d. coloured, gilt edges.

A Sequel to Mamma's Bible Stories.

Fifth Edition. Twelve Illustrations. 2s. 6d. cloth, 3s. 6d. coloured.

Scripture Histories for Little Children.

With Sixteen Illustrations, by JOHN GILBERT. Super-royal 16mo, price 3s. cloth; 4s. 6d. coloured, gilt edges.

CONTENTS.—The History of Joseph—History of Moses—History of our Saviour—The Miracles of Christ.

Sold separately: 6d. each, plain; 1s. coloured.

Bible Scenes;

Or, Sunday Employment for very young Children. Consisting of Twelve Coloured Illustrations on Cards, and the History written in Simple Language. In a neat box, 3s. 6d.; or the Illustrations dissected as a Puzzle, 6s. 6d.

FIRST SERIES: JOSEPH.   SECOND SERIES: OUR SAVIOUR.
THIRD SERIES: MOSES.   FOURTH SERIES: MIRACLES OF CHRIST.

"It is hoped that these 'Scenes' may form a useful and interesting addition to the Sabbath occupations of the Nursery. From their very earliest infancy little children will listen with interest and delight to stories brought thus palpably before their eyes by means of illustration."—*Preface.*

THE FAVOURITE LIBRARY.

A Series of Works for the Young; each Volume with an Illustration by a well-known Artist.   Price 1s. cloth.

1. THE ESKDALE HERD BOY. By LADY STODDART.
2. MRS. LEICESTER'S SCHOOL. By CHARLES and MARY LAMB.
3. THE HISTORY OF THE ROBINS. By MRS. TRIMMER.
4. MEMOIR OF BOB, THE SPOTTED TERRIER.
5. KEEPER'S TRAVELS IN SEARCH OF HIS MASTER.
6. THE SCOTTISH ORPHANS. By LADY STODDART.
7. NEVER WRONG; or, THE YOUNG DISPUTANT; and "IT WAS ONLY IN FUN."
8. THE LIFE AND PERAMBULATIONS OF A MOUSE.
9. EASY INTRODUCTION TO THE KNOWLEDGE OF NATURE. By MRS. TRIMMER.
10. RIGHT AND WRONG. By the Author of "ALWAYS HAPPY."
11. HARRY'S HOLIDAY. By JEFFERYS TAYLOR.
12. SHORT POEMS AND HYMNS FOR CHILDREN.

The above may be had Two Volumes bound in One, at Two Shillings cloth, or 2s. 6d. gilt edges, as follows:—

1. LADY STODDART'S SCOTTISH TALES.
2. ANIMAL HISTORIES. THE DOG.
3. ANIMAL HISTORIES. THE ROBINS and MOUSE.
4. TALES FOR BOYS. HARRY'S HOLIDAY and NEVER WRONG.
5. TALES FOR GIRLS. MRS. LEICESTER'S SCHOOL and RIGHT AND WRONG.
6. POETRY AND NATURE. SHORT POEMS and TRIMMER'S INTRODUCTION.

ILLUSTRATED BY GEORGE CRUIKSHANK.

Kit Bam, the British Sinbad;

Or, the Yarns of an Old Mariner. By MARY COWDEN CLARKE, author of "The Concordance to Shakspeare," etc. Fcap. 8vo, price 3s. 6d. cloth; 4s. gilt edges.

Aunt Jane's Verses for Children.

By Mrs. T. D. CREWDSON. Illustrated with twelve beautiful Engravings. Fcap. 8vo; 3s. 6d. cloth, gilt edges.

"A charming little volume, of excellent moral and religious tendency."—*Evangelical Magazine.*

NEW AND CHEAPER EDITION.

The Ladies' Album of Fancy Work.

Consisting of Novel, Elegant, and Useful Patterns in Knitting, Netting, Crochet, and Embroidery, printed in Colours. Bound in a beautiful cover. New Edition. Post 4to, 3s. 6d., gilt edges.

Visits to Beechwood Farm;

Or, Country Pleasures. By CATHERINE M. A. COUPER. Illustrations by ABSOLON. Small 4to, 3s. 6d., plain; 4s. 6d. coloured; gilt edges.

"The work is well calculated to impress upon the minds of the young the superiority of simple and natural pleasures over those which are artificial."—*Englishwoman's Magazine.*

The Modern British Plutarch;

Or, Lives of Men distinguished in the recent History of our Country for their Talents, Virtues and Achievements. By W. C. TAYLOR, LL.D. Author of "A Manual of Ancient and Modern History," etc. 12mo, Second Thousand, with a new Frontispiece. 4s. 6d. cloth; 5s. gilt edges.

"A work which will be welcomed in any circle of intelligent young persons."—*British Quarterly Review.*

Stories of Julian and his Playfellows.

Written by HIS MAMMA. With Four Illustrations by JOHN ABSOLON. Second Edition. Small 4to., 2s. 6d., plain; 3s. 6d., coloured, gilt edges.

"The lessons taught by Julian's mamma are each fraught with an excellent moral."—*Morning Advertiser.*

The Nine Lives of a Cat;

A Tale of Wonder. Written and Illustrated by C. H. BENNETT. Twenty-four Engravings. Imperial 16mo. price 2s. cloth; 2s. 6d. coloured.

"Rich in the quaint humour and fancy that a man of genius knows how to spare for the enlivenment of children."—*Examiner.*

Maud Summers the Sightless:

A Narrative for the Young. Illustrated by Absolon. 3s. 6d. cloth; 4s. 6d. coloured, gilt edges.

"A touching and beautiful story."—*Christian Treasury.*

The Celestial Empire;

or, Points and Pickings of Information about China and the Chinese. By the late "Old Humphrey." With Twenty Engravings from Drawings by W. H. Prior. Fcap. 8vo, 3s. 6d., cloth; 4s. gilt edges.

"The book is exactly what the author proposed it should be, full of good information, good feeling, and good temper."—*Allen's Indian Mail.*

London Cries and Public Edifices.

Illustrated in Twenty-four Engravings by Luke Limner; with descriptive Letter-press. Square 12mo, 2s. 6d. plain; 5s. coloured. Bound in emblematic cover.

The Silver Swan;

A Fairy Tale. By Madame de Chatelain. Illustrated by John Leech. Small 4to, 2s. 6d. cloth; 3s. 6d. coloured, gilt edges.

A Word to the Wise;

Or, Hints on the Current Improprieties of Expression in Writing and Speaking. By Parry Gwynne. 10th Thousand. 18mo. price 6d. sewed, or 1s. cloth. gilt edges.

"All who wish to mind their p's and q's should consult this little volume."—*Gentleman's Magazine.*

"May be advantageously consulted by even the well-educated."—*Athenæum.*

Tales from the Court of Oberon.

Containing the favourite Histories of Tom Thumb, Graciosa and Percinet, Valentine and Orson, and Children in the Wood. With Sixteen Illustrations by Alfred Crowquill. Small 4to, 2s. 6d. plain; 3s. 6d. coloured.

Rhymes of Royalty.

The History of England in Verse, from the Norman Conquest to the reign of Queen Victoria; with an Appendix, comprising a summary of the leading events in each reign. Fcap. 8vo, with Frontispiece. 2s. 6d. cloth.

True Stories from Ancient History,

Chronologically arranged from the Creation of the World to the Death of Charlemagne. Twelfth Edition. With 24 Steel Engravings. 12mo, 5s. cloth.

True Stories from Modern History,

Chronologically arranged from the Death of Charlemagne to the present Time. Eighth Edition. With 24 Steel Engravings. 12mo, 5s. cloth.

Mrs. Trimmer's Concise History of England,

Revised and brought down to the present time by Mrs. MILNER. With Portraits of the Sovereigns in their proper costume, and Frontispiece by HARVEY. New Edition in One Volume. 5s. cloth.

"The editing has been very judiciously done. The work has an established reputation for the clearness of its genealogical and chronological tables, and for its pervading tone of Christian piety."—*Church and State Gazette.*

Stories from the Old and New Testaments,

On an improved plan. By the Rev. B. H. DRAPER. With 48 Engravings. Fifth Edition. 12mo, 5s. cloth.

Wars of the Jews,

As related by JOSEPHUS; adapted to the Capacities of Young Persons, With 24 Engravings. Sixth Edition. 4s. 6d. cloth.

Pictorial Geography.

For the use of Children. Presenting at one view Illustrations of the various Geographical Terms, and thus imparting clear and definite ideas of their meaning. On a Large Sheet. Price 2s. 6d. in tints; 5s. on Rollers, varnished.

One Thousand Arithmetical Tests;

Or, The Examiner's Assistant. Specially adapted, by a novel arrangement of the subject, for Examination Purposes, but also suited for general use in Schools. By T. S. CAYZER, Head Master of Queen Elizabeth's Hospital, Bristol. Second Edition, revised and stereotyped. Price 1s. 6d. cloth.

⁎ Answers to the above, 1s. 6d. cloth.

One Thousand Algebraical Tests;

On the same plan. 8vo., price 3s. 6d. cloth.
Answers to the Algebraical Tests, price 2s. 6d. cloth.

THE ABBÉ GAULTIER'S GEOGRAPHICAL WORKS.

I. Familiar Geography.

With a concise Treatise on the Artificial Sphere, and two coloured Maps, illustrative of the principal Geographical Terms. Fifteenth Edition. 16mo, 3s. cloth.

II. An Atlas.

Adapted to the Abbé Gaultier's Geographical Games, consisting of 8 Maps coloured, and 7 in Outline, etc. Folio, 15s. half-bound.

Butler's Outline Maps, and Key;

Or, Geographical and Biographical Exercises; with a Set of Coloured Outline Maps; designed for the Use of Young Persons. By the late WILLIAM BUTLER. Enlarged by the author's son, J. O. BUTLER. Thirty-second Edition, revised. 4s.

Rowbotham's New and Easy Method of Learning

the FRENCH GENDERS. New Edition. 6d.

Bellenger's French Word and Phrase-book.

Containing a select Vocabulary and Dialogues, for the Use of Beginners. New Edition, 1s. sewed.

MARIN DE LA VOYE'S ELEMENTARY FRENCH WORKS.

Les Jeunes Narrateurs;

Ou Petits Contes Moraux. With a Key to the difficult words and phrases. Frontispiece. Second Edition. 18mo, 2s. cloth.
"Written in pure and easy French."—*Morning Post.*

The Pictorial French Grammar;

For the Use of Children. With Eighty Illustrations. Royal 16mo., price 1s. sewed; 1s. 6d. cloth.

Le Babillard.

An Amusing Introduction to the French Language. By a French Lady Seventh Edition. 2s. cloth.

Der Schwätzer;

Or, the Prattler. An amusing Introduction to the German Language, on the Plan of "Le Babillard." 16 Illustrations. 16mo, price 2s. cloth.

Battle Fields.

A graphic Guide to the Places described in the History of England as the scenes of such Events; with the situation of the principal Naval Engagements fought on the Coast of the British Empire. By Mr. WAUTHIER, Geographer. On a large sheet 3s. 6d.; in case 6s.; or on a roller, and varnished, 9s.

Tabular Views of the Geography and Sacred History

TORY of PALESTINE, and of the TRAVELS of ST. PAUL. Intended for Pupil Teachers, and others engaged in Class Teaching. By A. T. WHITE. Oblong 8vo, price 1s., sewed.

The First Book of Geography;

Specially adapted as a Text Book for Beginners, and as a Guide to the Young Teacher. By HUGO REID, author of " Elements of Astronomy," etc. Third Edition, carefully revised. 18mo, 1s. sewed.
" One of the most sensible little books on the subject of Geography we have met with." —*Educational Times.*

The Child's Grammar,

By the late LADY FENN, under the assumed name of Mrs. Lovechild. Forty-ninth Edition. 18mo, 9d. cloth.

The Prince of Wales' Primer.

With 300 Illustrations by J. GILBERT. Dedicated to her Majesty. New Edition, price 6d.; with title and cover printed in gold and colours, 1s.

Always Happy;

Or, Anecdotes of Felix and his Sister Serena. By the author of "Claudine," etc. Eighteenth Edition, with new Illustrations. Royal 18mo, price 2s. 6d. cloth.

Anecdotes of Kings,

Selected from History; or, Gertrude's Stories for Children. With Engravings. 2s. 6d. plain; 3s. 6d. coloured.

Bible Illustrations;

Or, a Description of Manners and Customs peculiar to the East, and especially Explanatory of the Holy Scriptures. By the Rev. B. H. DRAPER. With Engravings. Fourth Edition. Revised by J. KITTO, Editor of " The Pictorial Bible," etc. 3s. 6d. cloth.

The British History briefly told,
and a Description of the Ancient Customs, Sports, and Pastimes of the English. Embellished with Portraits of the Sovereigns of England in their proper Costumes, and 18 other Engravings. 3s. 6d. cloth.

Chit-chat;
Or, Short Tales in Short Words. By the author of "Always Happy." New Edition. With Eight Engravings. Price 2s. 6d. cloth, 3s. 6d. coloured, gilt edges.

Conversations on the Life of Jesus Christ.
For the use of Children. By a MOTHER. A new Edition. With 12 Engravings. 2s. 6d. plain; 3s. 6d. coloured.

Cosmorama.
The Manners, Customs, and Costumes of all Nations of the World described. By J. ASPIN. New Edition with numerous Illustrations. 3s. 6d. plain; and 4s. 6d. coloured.

Easy Lessons;
Or, Leading-Strings to Knowledge. New Edition, with 8 Engravings. 2s. 6d. plain; 3s. 6d. coloured, gilt edges.

Key to Knowledge;
Or, Things in Common Use simply and shortly explained. By a MOTHER, Author of "Always Happy," etc. Thirteenth Edition. With Sixty Illustrations. 3s. 6d. cloth.

Facts to correct Fancies;
Or, Short Narratives compiled from the Biography of Remarkable Women. By a MOTHER. With Engravings, 3s. 6d. plain; 4s. 6d. coloured.

Fruits of Enterprise;
Exhibited in the Travels of Belzoni in Egypt and Nubia. Thirteenth Edition, with six Engravings by BIRKET FOSTER. 18mo, price 3s. cloth.

The Garden;
Or, Frederick's Monthly Instructions for the Management and Formation of a Flower Garden. Fourth Edition. With Engravings of the Flowers in Bloom for each Month in the Year, etc. 3s. 6d. plain; or 6s. with the Flowers coloured.

How to be Happy;
Or, Fairy Gifts: to which is added a Selection of Moral Allegories. With Steel Engravings. Price 3s. 6d. cloth.

Infantine Knowledge.
A Spelling and Reading Book, on a Popular Plan, combining much Useful Information with the Rudiments of Learning. By the Author of "The Child's Grammar." With numerous Engravings. Tenth Edition. 2s. 6d. plain; 3s. 6d. coloured, gilt edges.

The Ladder to Learning.
A Collection of Fables, Original and Select, arranged progressively in words of One, Two, and Three Syllables. Edited and improved by the late Mrs. TRIMMER. With 79 Cuts. Nineteenth Edition. 3s. 6d. cloth.

Little Lessons for Little Learners.
In Words of One Syllable. By Mrs. BARWELL. Tenth Edition, with numerous Illustrations. 2s. 6d. plain; 3s. 6d. coloured, gilt edges.

The Little Reader.
A Progressive Step to Knowledge. Fourth Edition with sixteen Plates. Price 2s. 6d. cloth.

Mamma's Lessons.
For her Little Boys and Girls. Thirteenth Edition, with eight Engravings. Price 2s. 6d. cloth; 3s. 6d. coloured, gilt edges.

The Mine;
Or, Subterranean Wonders. An Account of the Operations of the Miner and the Products of his Labours; with a Description of the most important in all parts of the World. By the late Rev. ISAAC TAYLOR. Sixth Edition, with numerous corrections and additions by Mrs. LOUDON. With 45 new Woodcuts and 16 Steel Engravings. 3s. 6d. cloth.

Rhoda;
Or, The Excellence of Charity. Fourth Edition. With Illustrations. 16mo, 2s. cloth.

The Rival Crusoes,
And other Tales. By AGNES STRICKLAND, author of "The Queens of England." Sixth Edition. 18mo, price 2s. 6d. cloth.

Short Tales.
Written for Children. By DAME TRUELOVE and her Friends. A new Edition, with 20 Engravings. 3s. 6d. cloth.

The Students;
Or, Biographies of the Grecian Philosophers. 12mo, price 2s. 6d. cloth.

Stories of Edward and his little Friends.
With 12 Illustrations. Second Edition. 3s. 6d. plain; 4s. 6d. coloured.

Sunday Lessons for little Children.
By Mrs. BARWELL. Third Edition. 2s. 6d. plain; 3s. coloured.

The Grateful Sparrow.
A True Story, with Frontispiece. Third Edition. Price 6d. sewed.

How I Became a Governess.
By the Author of "The Grateful Sparrow." Third Edition. With Frontispiece. Price 2s. cloth, 2s. 6d. gilt edges.

Dicky Birds.
A True Story. By the same Author. With Frontispiece. Price 6d.

Dissections for Young Children;
In a neat box. Price 5s. each.

    1. SCENES FROM THE LIVES OF JOSEPH AND MOSES.

    2. SCENES FROM THE HISTORY OF OUR SAVIOUR.

    3. OLD MOTHER HUBBARD AND HER DOG.

    4. LIFE AND DEATH OF COCK ROBIN.

ONE SHILLING AND SIXPENCE EACH, CLOTH.

TRIMMER'S (MRS.) OLD TESTAMENT LESSONS. With 40 Engravings.	TRIMMER'S (MRS.) NEW TESTAMENT LESSONS. With 40 Engravings.

ONE SHILLING EACH. CLOTH.

THE DAISY, with Thirty Wood Engravings. (1s. 6d. coloured.) PRINCE LEE BOO.	THE COWSLIP, with Thirty Engravings. (1s. 6d. coloured.) THE CHILD'S DUTY.

DURABLE NURSERY BOOKS,

MOUNTED ON CLOTH WITH COLOURED PLATES,

ONE SHILLING EACH.

1 Alphabet of Goody Two-Shoes.	9 Mother Hubbard.
2 Cinderella.	10 Monkey's Frolic.
3 Cock Robin.	11 Old Woman and her Pig.
4 Courtship of Jenny Wren.	12 Puss in Boots.
5 Dame Trot and her Cat.	13 Tommy Trip's Museum of Birds,
6 History of an Apple Pie.	Part I.
7 House that Jack built.	14 ——————————— Part II.
8 Little Rhymes for Little Folks.	

DURABLE BOOKS FOR SUNDAY READING.

SCENES FROM THE LIVES OF JOSEPH AND MOSES. Illustrated by J. GILBERT. Printe on linen. Price 6d.

SCENES FROM THE LIFE OF OUR SAVIOUR. Illustrated by J. GILBERT. Printed on linen. Price 6d.

DARNELL'S EDUCATIONAL WORKS.

The attention of all interested in the subject of Education is invited to these Works, now in extensive use throughout the Kingdom, prepared by Mr. Darnell, a Schoolmaster of many years' experience.

1. COPY BOOKS.—A SHORT AND CERTAIN ROAD TO A GOOD HANDWRITING, gradually advancing from the Simple Stroke to a superior Small-hand.

LARGE POST, Sixteen Numbers, 6d. each.

FOOLSCAP, Twenty Numbers, to which are added Three Supplementary Numbers of Angular Writing for Ladies, and One of Ornamental Hands. Price 3d. each.

₊ This series may also be had on very superior paper, marble covers, 4d. each.

"For teaching writing I would recommend the use of Darnell's Copy Books. I have noticed a marked improvement wherever they have been used."—*Report of Mr. Maye (National Society's Organizer of Schools) to the Worcester Diocesan Board of Education.*

2. GRAMMAR, made intelligible to Children, price 1s. cloth.

3. ARITHMETIC, made intelligible to Children, price 1s. 6d. cloth.

₊ Key to Parts 2 and 3, price 1s. cloth.

4. READING, a Short and Certain Road to, price 6d. cloth.

GRIFFITH AND FARRAN, CORNER OF ST. PAUL'S CHURCHYARD.

WERTHEIMER AND CO., CIRCUS PLACE, FINSBURY CIRCUS.

CPSIA information can be obtained at www.ICGtesting.com
Printed in the USA
LVOW13*1346261013

358737LV00004B/57/P